Duquesne Studies

LANGUAGE AND LITERATURE SERIES

VOLUME SIX

GENERAL EDITOR:

Albert C. Labriola, *Department of English, Duquesne University*

EDITORIAL BOARD:

Divine Word

The Dialogue in Heaven, *Paradise Lost*, Book III
(Gustave Doré)

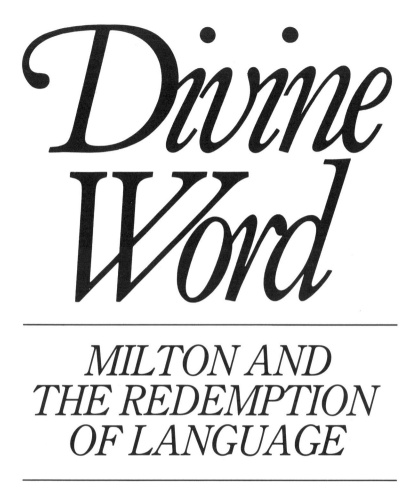

Divine Word

MILTON AND THE REDEMPTION OF LANGUAGE

by Robert L. Entzminger

DUQUESNE UNIVERSITY PRESS
Pittsburgh, PA

Published in the United States of America
by Duquesne University Press
600 Forbes Avenue, Pittsburgh, PA 15282

First Edition

Library of Congress Cataloging in Publication Data

Entzminger, Robert L., 1948–
    Divine word.

    Bibliography: p.
    Includes index.
    1. Milton, John, 1608–1674—Style.   2. Christian poetry,
English—History and criticism.   3. Speech in literature.
4. Temptation in literature.   5. Fall of man in literature.
6. Redemption in literature.   7. Rhetoric—1500–1800.
I. Title.
PR3594.E57   1985   821'.4   84–28799
ISBN 0-8207-0172-6

For Mary Lou

─────────────

Eloquence firste given by God, and after loste
by manne, and laste repaired by GOD again.

—Thomas Wilson,
The Arte of Rhetorique (1582)

Contents

I   Introduction: The Ruins of Babel in Seventeenth-
Century England   1

I   "Prompt Eloquence": Edenic Speech and
the Book of Nature   21

II   "Barbarous Dissonance": The Epic War
of Words   43

III   Michael, Adam, and the Means of Revelation   72

IV   Recovering the Word: The Ethics of Intention
and the Warrant for Action in *Comus* and
Paradise Regained   91

V   Responding to the Word: The Narrator in
Paradise Lost   119

VI   *Samson Agonistes* and the "Trivial Weapon"
of Words   145

Conclusion: From Babel to Pentecost   168

Notes   171

Index   185

Acknowledgements

At a time when literary scholars generally may be excused for finding themselves fallen on evil days, it is both pleasing and humbling to reflect on my own good fortune as I note, if only partially, the immense debts I have incurred in bringing this study to fruition. I must first of all acknowledge the inspiration and example of fine teachers at Washington and Lee University and Rice University. I am particularly grateful to Stewart A. Baker, Charles Garside, Jr., and the late John E. Parish, all of Rice, for keeping my wandering within bounds as I explored simultaneously the complexities of Milton, Milton scholarship, and Reformation theology.

I have attempted to document, as scrupulously as possible, the extent to which the work of other Miltonists has enabled my own, but footnotes cannot indicate the importance of the generous encouragement I received at crucial times from Georgia Christopher, Stanley Fish, Joseph Summers, and especially Jason Rosenblatt, whose willingness to listen to my ideas and to share his own learning and critical insights saved me from countless errors of fact or judgment. My students and colleagues at Virginia Polytechnic Institute and State University have provided a stimulating and congenial environment in which to work, and the advice and support I have received from my department head, Arthur M. Eastman, from the associate head, Hilbert H. Campbell, and from Ann Heidbreder Eastman have been invaluable. I must claim sole responsibility for the deficiencies that remain in the study; whatever virtues of coherence and precision it possesses are due in large part to the patience, sharp eyes, and good judgment of those who read and commented upon successive drafts: Christopher Clausen of Virginia Tech, James A. Freeman of the University of Massachusetts at Amherst, and the readers of Duquesne University Press.

Although I laid much of the groundwork for this study under the auspices of a graduate fellowship from Rice University, it would never have been completed without the additional assistance of a summer grant from the Center for Programs in the Humanities at Virginia Tech, which provided the means for me to examine seventeenth-century materials otherwise inaccessible. A fellowship from the National Endowment for the Humanities allowed me the time to complete the first draft, and the dean's office of Virginia Tech's College of Arts and Sciences provided me with the expert typing of Rebecca Cox. I have availed myself of the resources, in material and personnel, of several libraries, most frequently the Newman Library at Virginia Tech, the Library of Congress, and especially the Folger Shakespeare Library, among whose riches is the community of scholars it attracts. For permission to reprint those portions of this book that have appeared as articles, I wish to thank the editors of *English Literary Renaissance*, *Milton Studies*, and *Studies in English Literature 1500–1900*.

The dedication indicates, but expresses with least adequacy, the most pervasive debt of all.

Introduction

The Ruins of Babel in Seventeenth-Century England

WHEN Adam falls in *Paradise Lost*, so does his language. In Genesis speech does not explicitly receive the taint of Original Sin until the Tower of Babel episode, but Milton's Adam forfeits at the Fall the insight into things that their Edenic names express, and thus his postlapsarian speech bears at most an external resemblance to the purity and clarity of innocent words. Whether dated from God's curse on the builders of the tower or from the Fall itself, however, the problem that Babel symbolizes was particularly compelling in seventeenth-century England. Early humanists and many Elizabethans had seen in the refinement of speech the means to rectify thought and manners as well, but in the growing turmoil under James and Charles, the concern for language seemed to many to be not a solution to the problem but one of its sources. To some religious reformers, verbal ornament simply distracts and confuses the soul in its quest for spiritual satisfaction. Scientists and rationalists shared this distrust, but while the pious sought to overcome the lures and uncertainties of human language through an appeal to the spirit, their secular counterparts reposed their faith in the quiddities of material reality. Like many of his contemporaries, Milton was acutely aware of the dangers inherent in verbal power, and he consistently acknowledged the superiority of reality, spiritual or material, to the human words with which it is conveyed. Yet for him the fact of the verbal fall does not lead

1

inevitably to the denigration of speech. Rather, along with most exponents of Reformation he found in the theology of the Word not the grounds for circumventing human language but the means for redressing the effects of Babel. Just as Original Sin had entailed the fall of speech, so spiritual and verbal redemption are linked.

Although a concept with such a long history is subject to various and often conflicting interpretations, Protestants in general followed Luther and Calvin, whose emphasis on the doctrine of the Word resulted in a reverence not only for Scripture but also for the preachers who expound and apply the biblical message. Guided by Augustine's attempt to enlist his Ciceronian training in the service of revealed religion, Protestant ministers undertook a self-conscious search for a style appropriate to their message. Religious poets of the seventeenth century, viewing their art as a complement to the ministerial vocation, shared the quest for an answerable style, and like the preachers and lyric poets, Milton attempted to forge a medium responsive to the demands of the Word as he perceived them. Recurrently he confronted in his poetry a series of adversaries whose greatest asset is their mastery of words, and through this encounter he was able not only to explore the nature of corrupt language but to define the terms on which verbal art can be redeemed, the power of speech reclaimed from its demonic usurper to be enlisted in the service of the Word.

[I]

For Agrippa of Nettesheim, author of an early and influential attack on rhetoric and poetry, the verbal fall has been replicated throughout history, and many of Milton's antecedents and contemporaries found in their own time particularly gross examples of its recurrence.[1] Renaissance humanists, for instance, saw in the Scholastic form of education a language whose effect is to retard the recovery from Original Sin. Arguing that the unpleasant style and stultifying method of reasoning serve to imprison people within a definition of themselves too narrow to suit either social realities or spiritual needs, they turned to the eloquence of

Cicero and Quintilian for the means to repair the ruins of our first parents. But in making language both the object and the instrument of reform, humanists at the same time invited attack from those who shared their ends but distrusted the means they chose to realize their goals. The opposition to rhetorical study first expressed itself in religious terms, but by the seventeenth century much the same argument was advanced on grounds of secular philosophy. While these two camps diverged on many issues, they agreed that the fascination with words is an important source of error, and thus that the attempt to correct through rhetoric the misplaced values of medieval theology is a remedy that seeks to cure the disease by perpetuating its cause.

Those who grounded in religion their attack on the cultivation of verbal art held that the human mind is too fundamentally depraved to entrust it with so powerful a weapon as eloquence. Finding in the obscurity of the Schoolmen a less threatening example of fallen speech than the suasive force the rhetoricians sought to unleash, these opponents of rhetoric argued that the only way to rectify the verbal fall is to avoid as much as possible the potential in words for ambiguity and deception. Secular literature, because it provides the readiest source for examples of misused eloquence, became, then, a convenient target for vitriolic attack. Summoning the popular romances and the public stage to bear witness, the prosecution charged that the pursuit of verbal ornament is too frequently undertaken at the expense of the moral training required to use the skill properly, and the result is an art which employs its powers to glorify carnal love or equally profane topics. Apologists for poetry were willing to concede that though true eloquence is the apparel best suited to virtue, nonetheless vice may occasionally dress itself in borrowed robes. But to their opponents the subject matter is incidental; it simply manifests the corruption that inheres in the skill itself. While the campaign against literature is usually identified with Puritan extremists such as William Prynne, the nominally Catholic Agrippa is illustrative of an attitude that gained increasing currency in seventeenth-century England. "The Poete," he complains, "had lieffer to halt in his life then in his Verse," and he defines poesy as

an Arte, that was devised to no other ende, but to please the
eares of foolishe men, with wanton Rithmes, with measures,
and weightinesse of sillables, and with a vaine jarringe of
wordes, and to deceive mens mindes, with the delectation of
fables, and with fardels of lies.[2]

To Agrippa as to many of his successors, it is not just the ends
the poetry serves but its distracting appeal to the senses that
makes it suspect, and thus the more its defenders celebrated the
powers of literature, the more they confirmed the fears of their
opponents.

Consequently the faults of eloquence cannot be mitigated
simply by recruiting it for the pulpit. Ministers who employed
the learned, elaborate style of preaching popular in the seventeenth century became liable to the same charge of verbal
idolatry implicit in Agrippa's castigation of poets: they create an
artifice that diverts attention from the reality of God. For some
extremists, this possibility requires us to eschew any sort of
calculation in speech. William Dell for instance counseled preachers not to prepare sermons but to await the inspiration of the
Holy Spirit. And finally, wearied perhaps by an endless succession of voices contending for allegiance, some Protestants abandoned words themselves, hoping no longer to reform the world
but only to transcend it. Ranters and Quakers among others
found in the intimations of the unspoken, inner Word a message
that renders articulate human speech and even Scriptures obsolete.

The religious polemic against verbal art registered an impact
on preaching style and church services, but its most spectacular
triumph came with the closing of the theaters during the Inter-
regnum. Though the Restoration reopened the playhouses and
welcomed poets at court, the campaign against all forms of
eloquence in some ways intensified in the late seventeenth century, its vanguard passing from the custody of pious zealots to
the rationalists of the Royal Society. The Anglican divine Joseph
Glanvill, wishing to persuade the society that he has repented for
the elaborate preaching style he had once cultivated, argues for
simplicity and clarity from the pulpit in much the same terms
that dissenting ministers had used earlier in the century:

we should speak, *not as pleasing men, but God*; with that
seriousness and gravity as becomes those that design to
persuade men, in the matters that relate to the glory of God,
and their own present, and future well-being: for which
purposes a manly unaffectedness and simplicity of speech is
most proper. There is a bastard kind of eloquence that is
crept into the Pulpit, which consists in affectations of wit and
finery, flourishes, metaphors, and cadencies . . . we must not
debase our great, and important message by those vanities of
conceited speech: plainness is for ever the best eloquence,
and 'tis the most forcible: so that our study should be to
represent what we have to deliver in proper, and easie
expressions; neglecting and despising all starchedness of set,
and affected speaking.[3]

Though Glanvill appears to be reviving the arguments of the
Puritans, however, neither he nor his Royal Society colleagues
were willing to endorse the results the program of their antecedents had produced. In fact the earlier reform of preaching was
found to be inadequate, having eliminated ornateness only to
leave a legacy of obfuscation.

Turning the cry for plainness against its authors, Restoration
England found the fall of language accelerating, or at least its
restitution hindered, as the consequence of the political and
religious wranglings of the Civil War. Among the traits Butler
satirizes in the Puritan Sir Hudibras are his pedantry and his
"Babylonish dialect." And in the same year as the first edition of
Milton's epic, the Royal Society's historian Thomas Sprat published a call for a new reformation of the English language,
which he claims was "still fashioning, and beautifying it self" in
an orderly development from Chaucer "down to the beginning of
our late *Civil Wars*." Responding to the need to express the "new
thoughts of men" that "such busie, and active times" engender,
however, the language had undergone during the war an expo-
nential growth, not all of it fruitful. For along with the addition
of "many sound, and necessary Forms, and Idioms, which it
before wanted," English suffered the introduction of "many
fantastical terms" from "our *Religious Sects*." Consequently Sprat
sought the establishment of an English Academy, which would

"set a mark on the ill Words; correct those, which are to be retained; admit, and establish the good; and make some emendations in the Accent, and Grammar"; and he also proposes an "*Impartial Court* of *Eloquence*; according to whose Censure, all Books, or Authors should either stand or fall."[4] Milton himself parodies, in the "Vain wisdom . . . and false Philosophie" (*PL*, II.565) of the theologically-disposed devils, the same abstract quibbling to which Butler and Sprat object.[5] But the linguistic fatigue which underlies Sprat's desire to institutionalize literary judgment has causes more fundamental than the impatience with theological jargon he shared with Milton; and despite its apparent compatibility with the religious attack on eloquence, the Royal Society's attitude toward language is based upon principles fundamentally different from those of its pious antecedents.

In the volatile climate of Reformation and Revolution, with their incessant and often successful challenges to institutions once thought divinely ordained, there developed alongside millennial optimism an uneasiness about all artificial realities, whether society itself or the common language on which social cohesion depends. As the inevitability of inherited social, political, and religious institutions came to seem less certain, so words began to seem equally unreliable. Underlying all the defenses of eloquence is the conviction that words are the instruments of knowledge, the reflections of a transcendent reality which they move us to seek. While religious reformers affirmed their faith in eternal verities, the antirhetorical extremists based their attack on the premise that words are an encumbrance, rhetorical strategies a detour through the Wood of Error in the quest for the fixity of absolute truth. But if religious objections are grounded in a Neoplatonic distrust of human inventions as a route to God, the Restoration establishment, having observed the social chaos attendant upon sectarian dispute, was uncomfortable as well in the intangible realm of the spirit. To be sure, many Royal Society members were ministers equally sincere in their vocations, and their writings reflect the continuing influence of Platonism, partly by way of Descartes. But unlike the more exclusively religious opposition, they were persuaded that human reason alone can rectify the fall of language, and their assumptions in many cases tend to include a large measure of Aristotle. Thus instead of seeking truth through transcendent experience, advocates of the scientific method focused their quest for certainty on the concrete reality of the natural world and the comfortably restrictive methods of rational inquiry.

It was, then, in an attempt to restore a sense of certitude to a disquieted world that the society undertook its program to make language the undistorting image of nature, the tractable messenger of reason. But while Restoration linguists diverged radically from their religious counterparts in their assumptions and goals, whether the starting point was theology or science, Plato or Aristotle, the campaign against eloquence was the result of an impulse to circumvent the ephemeral in the search for the absolute, and it argued that words serve only to obstruct our vision of the things for which they stand. In communicating either God or the quiddities of material nature, the best style seems to be no style, a means of expression remarkable only for its transparency.

[II]

The antirhetorical campaign was of course more absolute in principle than in application, and the call for plainness and clarity led finally to an eloquence of another kind. Influenced by Bacon and with an inherent distaste for Elizabethan copiousness, Jonson devised a Neoclassical style which reached fruition in Pope. Yet this contribution cannot obscure the fact that the philosophical attacks on verbal art succeeded in subordinating rhetoric to reason. Though religious reformers were equally vociferous in their polemics, however, most Protestants until well into the seventeenth century based their ideas about language on the soundness of the marriage between *sapientia et eloquentia* that secular linguists sought to put asunder. Like the apologists for poetry themselves, reforming preachers found in words not just a necessary means to disseminate their ideas but one that is divinely sanctioned.

The Protestant attitude toward language is difficult to define, in part because the question is usually discussed only in the context of other issues, in part because the Reformation attracted a constituency whose goals and backgrounds were widely varied. In general, though, the emphasis on human depravity that led some reformers to denounce eloquence in absolute terms suggested to most others that verbal facility ought to be cultivated. The basis for this conviction is the concept of the Word, a doctrine central to Protestantism and crucial to poets who like Milton sought to serve God through their art. *Logos* is a Neoplatonic concept which entered the Scriptures in the Gospel of St. John, where it serves to name the agent of God's creation and the medium for his revelation. As it is used there, however, it becomes transformed. For Neoplatonists the *Logos* is incorporeal, and temporal words are thus only an impediment in the quest for supernal reality. The religious assault on eloquence indicates that this position represents a persistent, sometimes powerful current of Christianity, but the narrow view of Platonism on which it is based ignores the broader Christian interpretation of the concept. Making the *Logos* incarnate, Christianity overcame the dualism between natural and supernatural, sanctifying the former as the means to achieve the latter. Thus, in its customary translation as "Word," the idea verifies the divine origin of language in the mind of God and provides the warrant for serving God in speech. Wisdom and eloquence are one.

Through the Middle Ages the concept was treated with different emphases, depending upon the needs of the particular time and the commitments of the individual author.[6] And if in the Renaissance the champions of rhetoric and poetry relied on it at least implicitly, nonetheless the doctrine was advanced most vigorously, its applications pursued with greatest diligence in the sixteenth and seventeenth centuries by exponents of the Reformation. As on many other issues, Protestants entrusted themselves on the subject of the Word to the guidance of St. Augustine. In much of his most influential work Augustine was concerned to establish a link between his Christianity and his training in Ciceronian rhetoric. The tension he felt between his longing for *sapientia* and his attraction to *eloquentia* he found resolved in Ambrose, under whose direction he became a catechumen in the Christian religion. Thus discovering an example for employing his profession in the service of his faith, he sought to justify this resolution by developing an epistemology and a theory of language based upon the concept of the Word. As it is progressively articulated in his works, Creation by the Word, and more fully the Incarnation of the Word, make the reality of God accessible to limited human minds. Supplementing the Scriptures with meditation and prayer, the mind employs verbal means to discover in its own tripartite structure an image of the Trinity.

In the *Confessions* Augustine comes to realize that God has led him to Ambrose so that Ambrose can lead him to God (V.13), and at the beginning of the work he discerns a similarly dialectical pattern between knowledge and prayer. Wondering which precedes the other, he resolves the issue by suggesting a relationship that is at once circular and progressive:

> For how can one pray to you unless one knows you? . . . Or is it rather the case that we should pray to you in order that we may come to know you? . . . Let me seek you, Lord, by praying to you and let me pray believing in you; since to us you have been preached. My faith prays to you, Lord, this faith which you gave me and with which you inspired me through the Incarnation of your Son and through the ministry of the preacher.[7]

Through the Word, God inspires faith, the beginning of knowledge, but the prayer thus evoked leads to an understanding ever more complete. "Thus," Augustine points out in *The Trinity*, "in that realm of eternal truth from which all things temporal were made, we behold with our mind's eye the pattern upon which our being is ordered, and which rules all to which we give effect with truth and reason, in ourselves or in the outer world. Thence we conceive a truthful knowledge of things, which we have within us as a kind of *word*, begotten by an inward speech."[8]

If through prayer one can achieve a knowledge of the Word, then through preaching one can communicate that knowledge to others. Even a sanctified rhetoric, however, has important limitations. Because they are only signs, words cannot impart a

direct knowledge of reality. Consequently the auditor can judge
the rectitude of verbal signs, their accurate representation of
their *significata*, only by a knowledge of reality and not simply by
a knowledge of language.[9] But despite the partiality of their
communicative function, words provide the best medium for
approaching God as well as an especially apt way to serve him.
Marcia Colish's summary of Augustine's position is particularly
illuminating:

> Augustine projected a redeemed rhetoric as the outcome of a
> revealed wisdom. On the basis of this theory, a twofold
> linguistic transformation was in order: the faculty of human
> speech was to be recast as a Pauline mirror, faithfully me-
> diating God to man in the present life; and the agencies
> appointed for the translation of man's partial knowledge by
> faith into his complete knowledge of God by direct vision
> were to be redefined as modes of verbal expression.[10]

Like Scripture itself, Augustine was cited in support of widely
divergent views in the Reformation, and Stanley Fish has
adopted one of these interpretations as the basis for his reading
of several seventeenth-century texts. Making no distinction between Platonic and Augustinian dialectic, Fish argues that both
work "not to persuade to a point, but to a vision in which all
points are one." As a result, the art depreciates itself: "Augustine, in effect, has made language defeat itself by making it point
away from the temporal-spatial vision it naturally reflects."[11]
But while the transcendent, Platonic vision may fulfill the quest,
it does not in most of Augustine's works negate the value of the
process by which we achieve it, a process sanctified by the
Word's incarnation.

Even if Fish is right in his reading of Augustine, however, his
extension of the self-consuming dialectic to the poetry and prose
of the seventeenth century overlooks the very different way in
which the more central Reformation thinkers interpreted Augustine's doctrine of the Word. On the Continent the leading
reformers emphasized repeatedly not just the primacy of the
inner voice but the importance of the interplay between external
words and the Word within. Luther's *Turmserlebnis*, his sudden

illumination while grappling with Romans 1:17, exemplifies perfectly the operation of the inner Word, but like the one Augustine describes in the *Confessions* (VIII.12), the insight is stimulated and reinforced by Scriptural revelation. As a result of this experience, Luther asserted the priority of the Bible and the individual conscience against the authority of the Church. For Luther "the most holy Word of God" is the only thing "necessary for Christian life, righteousness, and freedom," and by the Word he appears to understand both the biblical text and the inner voice that confirms the reality for which the Scriptures are a sign.[12]

Like the humanist attack on Scholasticism, the Reformation assault on medieval theology and liturgy is grounded in the conviction that the pursuit of verbal skill is a divine imperative. If, as Luther argues, people are basically depraved, then the logic-chopping of the dialecticians cannot induce faith, and the splendor of ritual and icon, through which the Church enhances its authority at God's expense, is an invitation to idolatry. By stripping the churches of their art and conducting simplified services in the vernacular, Protestants are able to concentrate their attention upon the more reliable guide of Scriptures and the minister who expounds them, feeling no need for a remote arbiter of the faith. But for Scriptures to be sufficient, the translations must be accurate and the faithful literate. Consequently Luther, in his plea for schools maintained by local governments, argues for a link between moral decay and the decline of verbal skills:

> And let us be sure of this: we will not long preserve the gospel without the languages. The languages are the sheath in which this sword of the Spirit is contained. . . . If through our neglect we let the languages go (which God forbid!), we shall not only lose the gospel, but the time will come when we shall be unable either to speak or write a correct Latin or German. As proof and warning of this, let us take the deplorable and dreadful example of the universities and monasteries, in which men have not only unlearned the gospel, but have in addition so corrupted the Latin and German languages that the miserable folk have been fairly

turned into beasts, unable to speak or write a correct German or Latin, and have wellnigh lost their natural reason to
boot. . . .

When our faith is thus held up to ridicule, where does the
fault lie? It lies in our ignorance of the languages; and there
is no other way out than to learn the languages.[13]

The doctrine Luther found congenial to his program of reform
and confirmed in his own religious experience Calvin made an
integral part of the systematic theology he devised for Protestantism. The *Institutes* are concerned primarily with the knowledge of God, and like Augustine Calvin insisted that the agency
of God's accommodation to humans is the Son, who is both the
creating Word and the incarnate Word. That God's revelation is
verbal Calvin emphasizes by translating the Greek *Logos* as *Sermo*
("Speech") in order to avoid the more limited connotations of
Verbum: "As to the Evangelist calling the Son of God *the Speech*,
the simple reason appears to me to be, first, because he is the
eternal Wisdom and Will of God; and, secondly, because he is
the lively image of His Purpose; for, as *Speech* is said to be among
men the image of the mind, so it is not inappropriate to apply
this to God, and to say that He reveals himself to us by his
Speech."[14] Like the rhetoricians, Calvin found *ratio* implicit in
oratio, wisdom and eloquence indissolubly joined.

Preferring the word to the image, Calvin exalted both the
Scriptures and the preachers who expound them, and he rel-
egated the sacraments to a position less important than the one
they occupy in Catholicism. In his theology only baptism and
the Eucharist retain their sacramental character, and he shifted
the locus of the union between God and the participants from the
ceremony and its elements to the word which makes its meaning
clear. By God's free action, his minister may become an effec-
tual vehicle for communicating divine truth, the human word
transformed to the Word of God. In this way, as Ronald Wallace
has said, "a relationship is set up between the human act of the
preacher and the divine action of grace which we may call a
sacramental union."[15] For Calvin as for Luther and Augustine,
knowledge of God is the result of an interaction between external
words and the living Word within.

Thus the leaders of the Continental Reformation, while insisting upon the importance of the silent, inner Word, continued to affirm the value of written and spoken words. In fact, the reliance upon conscience and introspection makes the Scriptures doubly important, for seeking truth in the recesses of the fallen mind requires an objective, Scriptural test as the means to distinguish illumination from passion, true prophecy from false. Although for the individual the letter of the text is dead without the confirmation of the Holy Spirit, the revelation received in this way must conform to the testimony of the Bible or it is to be rejected as inspired by Satan. And if the human inclination to mistake the workings of one's own passions for divine impulse makes the touchstone of Scriptures indispensable, the fallenness of the hearers requires the preacher's greatest efforts in seeking to move them. Balancing the test of Scriptures against the testimony of the Spirit, countering the gnostic potential of the reverence for prophecy with an insistence upon scholarship, clarity, and rhetorical effectiveness, the doctrine of the Word establishes an equilibrium between goal and process. While it continues to be subject to narrower interpretation, in this form it provides both a compelling eschatology and an affirmation of the journey, a veneration for the eternal, unspoken Word coupled with a practical reliance upon the temporal, external words through which it is evoked, tested, reinforced.

Imported into England, the doctrine of the Word retained for the most part its emphasis on the association between the divine Logos and human speech. At least early on in the seventeenth century, complaints about the ornate preaching style were not confined to dissenters, and the style itself was not the exclusive property of conservatives in the Church of England. But even if we accept the conflict as gradually polarizing into Anglican and Puritan camps, we must recognize that, perhaps more than other Protestants, dissenters were forced to rely upon verbal skills, and so their attacks on eloquence are themselves based on rhetorical considerations. Their criticism of the allusive and elaborate preaching style turns not upon whether to cultivate verbal skills but simply on the most effective strategy to pursue. Advocating a style they call "spiritual," "plain and perspicuous," Puritans developed an eloquence of their own, an artistry designed to appeal to the congregations whose support they sought. "The result," William Haller observes, "was a modified but not less imaginative style arising naturally out of medieval and Elizabethan practices in response to the needs and tastes of the audiences upon which the preachers depended for personal support as well as for the eventual triumph of their cause. The preachers, if they wished to survive, had to find means to stir imaginations, induce emotional excitement, wring the hearts of sinners, win souls to the Lord, in other words make themselves understood and felt."[16]

Like their fellow Protestants, then, Puritans showed a primary concern for moving their hearers and a conviction that they must rely upon the power of words to that end. Their polemics to the contrary notwithstanding, the practice of most dissenting ministers reveals that they did not object to eloquence itself but only to the confusion of ends that emphasizes ornamentation at what they conceived to be the expense of the audience's understanding. William Perkins, for example, acknowledged that the preacher must call upon all possible erudition in preparing a sermon but must conceal that learning in the delivery in order to avoid distracting or confusing the congregation.[17] With dedicated rhetoricians and poets, the Puritan preacher "was quite prepared to use anything he knew as means to his end, but the end was to make everybody feel the force and reality of what he was saying."[18]

Criticisms about preaching style, then, had the effect and frequently the intent of redefining eloquence, not silencing it. Similarly the campaign against poetry, though it succeeded in closing the theaters temporarily, had a more profound impact on the literature that continued to be produced. The power that makes poetry so formidable an adversary makes it an equally desirable ally. As Agrippa shows that the distrust of literature is not limited to Protestants, George Wither reveals that the attitude is not characteristic even of all Puritans. In the preface to his translation of the Psalms, Wither defends poetic art as a divine invention whose capacity for demonic abuse does not preclude its service in a holy cause:

the Divell went further: and as he had imitated God in his
sacrifices; so he also followed that example, in delivering his
Oracles in *Verse*: as at *Delphos*, and else-where. But as the
abhominations which were used in the sacrifices of the
Gentiles, were no cause of abolishing the sacrifices of the
Jewes, before their appointed time: or as the delivery of the
Divels cousenages in *verse*, was no reason why the holy
Oracles of the true God should be neglected: So, there is no
cause why *Verse* and divine *Poesie*, should grow into contempt, because the world hath made use of it to her owne
purposes.[19]

But reforming the subject which eloquence serves does not fully
meet the objections of its detractors; there must be as well a
reform of style.

Like the preachers who sought to purify pulpit oratory, religious poets urged simplicity and straightforwardness as the style
appropriate to a divine subject. Wither, for instance, warns his
readers, "although florishes of Art, and deep schoolepoynts,
gained greatest applause, amongst those which gloried in the
aboundance of curious knowledges: yet one Treatise compiled
after that simple manner, which to this wise age seems foolish,
makes many times mo good Christians, then a thousand volumes
stuffed with most applauded learnings."[20] Similarly George Herbert seems, in the "Jordan" poems, to enjoin with Sidney's muse
the pursuit of a simple, honest style. But the call for plainness in
poetry as in preaching betrays for the most part a contempt
simply for the cultivation of an elaborate style for its own sake.
Just as the Royal Society linguists hoped to bring words strictly
to the heel of their referents, some religious detractors of eloquence actually seem to mean what they say. But most Protestants, as Barbara Lewalski has recently demonstrated, sought
only to correct the abuses of literary art and to make pulpit
oratory a more effective vehicle for its divine message.[21] The
conscious attention to artistry in Herbert's verse, like Wither's
praise of poetry, suggests that he is making clear not so much his
suspicion of art as the fact that he is practicing a poetry consecrated to God and not to itself.

[III]

Pursuing his vocation at a time when eloquence was subject to distrust and language itself to reexamination, Milton was intensely conscious of the dangers of verbal art when used irresponsibly or sought for its own sake. Even though the curriculum he sets forth in *Of Education* takes its structure and much of its content from literature, he defers the study of logic and rhetoric until his students acquire the wisdom to use them properly. The goal of his program is to produce statesmen and ministers whose leadership, manifested in speaking and writing "in every excellent matter," is predicated upon their "universall insight into things" (CPW, 2: 406).[22] By the same token he pledges himself early on in his career "to fix all the industry and art I could unite to the adorning of my native tongue," but he pursues his goal "not to make verbal curiosities the end, that were a toylsom vanity, but to be an interpreter and relater of the best and sagest things among mine own Citizens" (*RCG*; CPW, 1: 811-812). With the detractors of eloquence he finds the subject, not the means of its expression, to be the defining element in communication. As faith is the form of good works, so according to the *Art of Logic*, "The form or true cause of an art is not so much the methodical arrangement of those precepts as it is the teaching of some useful matter; for an art is what it is rather because of what it teaches than because of its method of teaching" (CE, 11: 9). Subordinating the sign to its referent, however, does not entail the nostalgia for a linguistic Eden represented by the members of the Royal Society. Perhaps more fully than the opponents of verbal art, Milton recognized the dangers arising from the corruption of language, but he also realized that it can serve as the medium of God's revelation only if its full powers are exploited.

As a theologian Milton was sufficiently idiosyncratic to make any attempt at categorizing him extraordinarily difficult. In the *Christian Doctrine*, however, he followed Calvin's preference for *Sermo* over *Verbum* as the more accurate rendering of *Logos* (CPW, 6: 239).[23] More important, as a poet he adhered to the central Protestant doctrine of the Word and employed it, against the approach to language offered by secular philosophers and some religious extremists, to justify his vocation and to define the means of pursuing it. Like Luther, he posited a close relationship between language and morality. In a letter to Benedetto Buonmattei he asserts,

> when speech is partly awkward and pedantic, partly inaccurate and badly pronounced, what does it say but that the souls of the people are slothful and gaping and already prepared for any servility? On the other hand, not once have we heard of an empire or state not flourishing at least moderately as long as it continued to have pride in its Language, and to cultivate it. (CPW, 1: 329-330)

And although he acknowledges the priority of moral training in *Of Education*, he is equally emphatic in securing for verbal art an exalted position in his curriculum. Because he believes the minister or statesman must understand the poet's art before he can master his own, his proposal for educating aspirants to these professions aims as one of its important goals to show the students "what Religious, what glorious and magnificent use might be made of Poetry both in divine and humane things" (*Ed*; CPW, 2: 405-406). But poetry is more than a prerequisite for entry into other professions; it is itself a vocation equal to that of church or government service. The poet's abilities, Milton declares in *The Reason of Church Government*, "are of power beside the office of a pulpit" (CPW, 1: 816), and in *Areopagitica* he asserts his claim upon Parliament's attention by citing the deference of the Athenian Senate to private citizens "who profest the study of wisdome and eloquence" (CPW, 2: 489). Fully confident of the poet's authority, Milton can consider, without either irony or an air of self-importance, whether epic or tragedy is the genre most appropriate for a poem "doctrinal and exemplary to a Nation" (*RCG*; CPW, 1: 815). Milton's poetry, then, is acutely self-conscious and implicitly polemical. Introduced in a climate of suspicion regarding eloquence, it acknowledges the limitations of language while at the same time finding in the Reformation theology of the Word the warrant for verbal art.

As he pursues his exploration of the nature of redeemed speech, Milton must repeatedly confront demonic or fallen speakers. That he defines his art almost always in response to an instance of its abuse is due in part to the embattled position of his calling in the seventeenth century, in part to the Scholastic method of education in which he was trained.[24] But the procedure also reflects his convictions about fallen epistemology. The Word of God may be approached not only through the dialectic between external and internal revelation, but also, and more typically in the postlapsarian world, through the effort to combat the words of false prophets. To him the curse of the Tree of Knowledge is that "we do not even know good except through evil" (*CD*; CPW, 6: 352). Although ontologically prior to evil, virtue is accessible to the fallen mind only through a confrontation with its opposite, for "that which purifies us is triall, and triall is by what is contrary" (*Areo*; CPW, 2: 515).

Thus Milton frequently indicates his self-consciousness about his poetry by reference to the evil counterpart against whose example the poem's speaker defines himself. The Nativity Ode implicitly contrasts the speaker's words, themselves a function of the Word whose incarnation they celebrate, with the silenced pagan oracles; and "Lycidas" among other things provides a rededication to poetry in the face of the dual challenge presented by death and the "blind mouths" of the false shepherds. But the struggle between good and evil speakers is realized most fully in the temptation poems. Whatever other vices the tempters may represent, they are dangerous because of their ability to distort our perception of reality by manipulating the words used to describe it. Resisting this effort with varying degrees of success are Milton's protagonists, through whose trials he explores and defines the course his epic narrator must follow as he seeks to convey his "higher Argument" (*PL*, IX.42).

Before he can clarify the nature of fallen speech and the terms on which it can be redeemed, Milton must first explore the language of Eden. And as Raphael in Book VIII acquaints Adam more fully with the relationship between signs and things in Paradise, so through the account of the War in Heaven he dramatizes how words can be detached from their referents, appearance and reality set at odds. In response to the ambiguity and polysemous quality with which language is tainted after the Fall, Milton in the last books seems to be reverting to the plain style for which preachers and other poets sometimes betray a nostalgia. But Michael is confronted with a special situation, a pupil who has lost the intellectual advantages of innocence without having yet acquired the means to deal with the circumstances his sin has brought about. Adam's presuppositions lead him to expect a consonance between appearance and reality the fallen world does not yield, and he must therefore be purged of his Edenic perspective while being educated to the typological structure of history through whose medium the Fall will become fortunate.

Like Adam at the end of *Paradise Lost,* Milton's other protagonists must also confront a world defined in part by the categories of fallen language and discover how to recast speech so that it can once again serve as a vehicle appropriate to convey divine revelation. For the poet the solution lies first in preparing himself to become God's agent, following a regimen similar to the one the Lady in *Comus* and Christ in *Paradise Regained* undergo. But preparation does not guarantee execution. In order for his aspirations to be realized, he must be infused with the Word, and as the result of this divine warrant he is free to exercise his creative powers to their fullest. The narrator of *Paradise Lost* seeks this kind of inspiration, and he offers his epic as evidence that he has received it. While some Protestants take God to sanction only the least elaborate, most transparent style, others including Milton find in the rich complexity of Creation the model for poetic art and the means to transform what is potentially confusing or deceptive into a medium for celebrating God's beneficence and justifying his ways. Although the pristine innocence of unfallen speech is incapable of being recovered, Babel can nonetheless be countered, its curse made fortunate not by restricting the function of words but by Pentecost, the dispensation which sanctifies the full resources of language for God's service.

Finally, *Samson Agonistes* recapitulates the importance of the doctrine of the Word and reaffirms the appropriateness of human language as an instrument capable of redeemed use. Like Adam, Samson resumes his heroic role by regaining on more sophisticated terms than previously his mastery of language. Attending to the inner Word, he fulfills his prophesied mission, but he does so because he becomes once more a riddler, deceiving his captors even as he expresses his total reliance upon God. As Milton defines the nature of true poetry by confronting its opposite, Samson learns how to be God's hero by rejecting the false images his visitors offer him, and he acquires the language necessary to express his knowledge by perfecting the weapon of words with which he refutes their positions.

CHAPTER ONE

"Prompt Eloquence"

Edenic Speech and the Book of Nature

I F the fall of language was a dominant problem in seventeenth-century England, Royal Society linguists prescribed as a solution the recovery of Edenic speech. The attitude of these scientists and philosophers toward language was paradoxical, for while they regarded conventional words as impediments to knowledge, they postulated a pristine language whose vocabulary would communicate its referents immediately. Likewise radical religious groups such as the Diggers had earlier sought to restore all of Creation to its original condition. Language would then become "pure," based solely on experience.[1] Confirming the speculations of linguists and preachers about Edenic speech, Milton's Adam speaks a language that seems almost to identify knowing and naming. When the creatures are brought before him, he recalls, "I nam'd them, as they pass'd, and understood / Thir Nature" (VIII.352-353). Even if we take the order in which he recounts the circumstances—naming before understanding—to suggest not causation but simultaneity, we must recognize that to Adam apprehending the name is inseparable from knowing the thing. Throughout *Paradise Lost* until the Fall, Adam displays his facility with signs, both verbal and natural, and the wisdom that accompanies this skill. But the language he employs, despite its purity and clarity, is not the precise and spare terminology of philosophic discourse; rather he celebrates his experiences and maintains marital harmony

through a special kind of poetic language. And as he offers
eloquence where the linguists hoped to find unadorned reason,
his pursuit of knowledge leads him not to rely more fully on his
intellect but to recognize the limits of the human mind in achieving answers to the questions he considers most urgent. Yet
through failure he finds unanticipated success, for the verbal
queries he addresses to the Creation, to God, and to Raphael
lead him always to greater self-knowledge and thus by an oblique
route to knowledge of God. Despite his innocence, then, Adam
acquires illumination much as his fallen heirs do, through the
dialectic between human words and the Word.

[I]

The language that seventeenth-century linguists imputed to
Adam and sought to recapture is both purely denotative and
admirably laconic. John Wilkins, among others, was confident
that a new language might be invented that would recover the
capacity of Adam's speech to disclose the natures of things
through their names. As a result of this reformed language, "we
should, by learning the *Character* and the *Names* of things, be
instructed likewise in their *Natures*, the knowledg of both which
ought to be conjoyned."[2] The desire to recover an Edenic
congruence between sign and referent similarly underlies Sprat's
praise of the Royal Society for encouraging a "Mathematical
plainness" of style, a return "to the primitive purity, and short-
ness, when men deliver'd so many *things*, almost in an equal
number of *words*."[3] But as the complexity and ambiguity of life in
the fallen world make this goal seem naive, so experience even in
Milton's Eden requires for its full statement a language capable
of more than plainness and brevity. Like the Cambridge Platonist Peter Sterry, Milton sees Adam as the first poet, expressing
his vision through a particular kind of wordplay and spontaneously celebrating his existence with a language that is stylized
and opulently redundant.[4]

If the verbal economy of the linguists' Paradise renders rhetoric in general suspect, then punning is surely forbidden fruit.

The Cambridge divine John Eachard cites "Punning, Quib-
ling, . . . and such other Delicacies of Wit" among the grounds
for the contempt in which the clergy was held, and Abraham
Cowley dismisses puns as inappropriate even in poetry.[5] Yet
puns are pervasive in *Paradise Lost*, and though they are commonly associated with Satan, they perform as well an especially
useful function in Eden. For while the reader perceives the world
dualistically, Adam is intuitively a monist, and so the language
he speaks involves a kind of punning in which the meanings are
mutually supportive, in contrast to the tension arising from, say,
Donne's sexual/religious puns. Thus in the wordplay with "Sole
partner"/"Part of my Soul" (IV.411, 487), Adam stresses both
Eve's singularity and the fact that each of them depends upon
and completes the other.[6] In a slightly different way, Adam's
inquiry to Raphael about angelic love also indicates the ability of
unfallen language to contain without tension the varieties of
fallen meaning. Assuring Raphael that his devotion to Eve is
within limits, Adam concludes,

> To Love thou blam'st me not, for Love thou say'st
> Leads up to Heav'n, is both the way and guide;
> Bear with me then, if lawful what I ask;
> Love not the heav'nly Spirits, and how thir Love
> Express they, by looks only, or do they mix
> Irradiance, virtual or immediate touch?   (VIII.612-617)

The exact symmetry of these repetitions, using "Love" as both
noun and verb first as applied to man and then to angels,
indicates the perfect concord in Adam's mind between the
emotion of love and its expression, and between spiritual and
sexual love. The epic voice can appropriate this kind of language
for special purposes, but the effect of Adam's un-self-conscious
use is all the more striking to the reader, who knows monism
only as an alternative to the dualistic vision the metaphor
overcomes.

Not only is Adam's language metaphoric; it is also ritualistic
and copious, a trait especially apparent in the elaborate epithets
customarily adorning Edenic discourse. C. S. Lewis finds the

epithets enhancing the ceremony and elevation for which he praises Milton's verse, but though this effect is certainly achieved, it seems to me not the only purpose behind Milton's use.[7] The naming and renaming that occur throughout the account of life in Eden serve to demonstrate that Adam and Eve's insight extends beyond the lower creatures to each other, and as a result of their mutual dependence, one cannot consider the nature of his spouse without being reminded of one's own identity as well. Eve first addresses Adam in terms which make explicit her subordination to him: "O thou for whom / And from whom I was form'd flesh of thy flesh, / And without whom am to no end, my Guide / And Head" (IV.440-443). And Adam receives her as his wife with an epithet which acknowledges, like the sole/soul puns, the extent to which they are one: "Bone of my Bone, Flesh of my Flesh, my Self / Before me; Woman is her Name, of Man / Extracted" (VIII.495-497). Not all the epithets are so elaborate, but they all serve the true purpose of ritual, which is to articulate, to make clear and accessible, the motives, roles, and relationships of the participants. To the unfallen couple, naming reveals the character of both self and other.[8]

The clarity and honesty reflected in the epithets provide the basis for the marital concord of Adam and Eve. Although in requesting a companion with whom to "converse," to enjoy "Social communication" (VIII.396, 429), Adam expects God to understand by "conversation" more than just the exchange of words, nonetheless, his choice of terms suggests that the other forms of relationship are predicated upon verbal intercourse.[9] "*Speech*," Ben Jonson points out, "is the Instrument of *Society*," and in *Paradise Lost* words both originate the embryonic community and serve to maintain it.[10] Raphael recognizes the image of their maker in Adam's speech as well as in his "comeliness" (VIII.222), and Adam likewise compliments Eve in her absence for the grace her words and actions express (VIII.600-604). But Eve is also, Arnold Stein notes, the result of "a collaboration in dialogue between the eternal mind and Adam's mind in its first sustained trial," a point she emphasizes in referring to Adam as her "Author" (IV.635).[11] And as Eve is the articulation of Adam's idea as he is of God's, so conversation seems to be the source of their greatest joy, the medium through which their love is given fullest expression. When Adam speaks, Eve turns him "all ear to hear" (IV.410), and "With thee conversing" (IV. 639), she tells him, she forgets all time, forsakes all other delights.

In Eden the congruence between the intention of words and their effect is at least occasionally perfect. After Eve describes her dream, Adam "cheer'd . . . his fair Spouse, and she was cheer'd" (V.129). The sufficiency Eve finds in Adam's words matches the fullness with which their thoughts are given expression. In Paradise no distance is allowed to develop between an idea and its manifestation in word and deed, no opening through which guile might intrude into their innocence. The work they perform in praise and gratitude is as spontaneous as the "various style" of their orisons is "Unmeditated" (V.146, 149), and the function of their hymns is at least in part to make fully intelligible the motives behind their labors. Similarly the courtliness of their love-language serves to articulate the dignity and spirituality inherent in the physical pleasures of "the Rites / Mysterious of connubial Love" (IV.742-743). But even when the emotion expressed is perturbation, as in Eve's reaction to her dream, or annoyance, as in the dispute over whether they should work apart, the fact that it is articulated removes its power to disrupt their happiness. A part of the innocence, surely, of Eve's behavior just prior to the Fall, as well as with the "curiosity" and "uxoriousness" Adam betrays in his conversation with Raphael, is the absence of calculation. There is no attempt to manipulate the auditor or to deceive, but only to reveal one's thoughts more fully.

Together with the clarity of their insights, the thoroughness with which they are able to articulate their thoughts serves as an index to the effectiveness of Edenic speech in maintaining the amity of Adam and Eve. But language, it is commonly agreed, is ordained not only as the basis for society but also as the means for celebrating God. Despite his conviction that the verbal fall is the source of all our woe, the Royalist divine Richard Allestree traces the benefits of civilization to the gift of speech and then stresses its equally seminal place in religion: "From all these excellent uses of it in respect of man, we may collect another in relation to God, that is, the *praising* and *magnifying* his goodness, as for all other effects of his bounty, so particularly that he hath given us language, and all the consequent advantages of it."[12] As Satan realizes too late, the purest act of gratitude rests in the verbal acknowledgment of the Creator's gifts: "a grateful mind / By owing owes not, but still pays, at once / Indebted and discharg'd" (IV.55-57). Adam and Eve on the other hand demonstrate their continued innocence by returning to the Word the words his beneficence inspires, and their richest, most opulent language is reserved for their hymns. Yet finally the most important of their insights, the clearest measure of their verbal skill, is the ability to confess the limits of their perception to see, of their speech to express, the extent of God's goodness. Celebrating the glories of Creation, they realize that the Creator is at best "dimly seen" in his works, that in himself his wonder is "Unspeakable" (V.157, 156).

[II]

Like words, the phenomena of Nature are also signs, and they exhibit the same capacities and limitations as verbal signs. Adam's speech can reflect his insight into things partly because Creation itself derives from the Word, and the verbal source of Nature continues to be apparent in the terms Milton's characters apply to it. God (VIII.317), Raphael (VII.591), and Adam (VIII.360) all define God's role in Creation as his authorship; Raphael calls the universe "the Book of God" (VIII.67); and Adam ascribes verbal characteristics to natural phenomena. Of the stars, he observes that "Spaces incomprehensible . . . Thir distance argues" (VIII.20-21), and his first self-reflective act is described in terms which emphasize that he is himself a part of the Book of Nature he reads: "Myself I then perus'd" (VIII.267). As if bearing witness to its origins, Nature at times becomes quite communicative, its sympathy with the human couple characteristically expressed as a verbal response to their actions. Celebrating their nuptials,

> . . . the Earth
> Gave sign of gratulation, and each Hill;
> Joyous the Birds; fresh Gales and gentle Airs
> Whisper'd it to the Woods, and from thir wings
> Flung Rose, flung Odors from the spicy Shrub,
> Disporting, till the amorous Bird of Night
> Sung Spousal, and bid haste the Ev'ning Star
> On his Hill top, to light the bridal Lamp. (VIII.513-520)

At Eve's fall, "Nature from her seat / Sighing through all her Works gave signs of woe" (IX.782-783), and as Adam sins, "Nature gave a second groan, / Sky low'r'd, and muttering Thunder, some sad drops / Wept" (IX.1001-1003).

The Book of Nature is of course a familiar *topos* in medieval and Renaissance literature, but one of the means Milton uses to communicate the reality of Eden is to insist upon the literal truth of ideas that in the fallen world have become at best metaphors, at worst cliches.[13] His readers may see in the pathetic fallacy, for instance, at first only a pastoral convention, but in recognizing that he applies its terms denotatively in *Paradise Lost*, we realize how distant we are from the unity of experience that makes the sympathy of Nature for humanity a matter of course. Although Eve is created to satisfy Adam's need for a mate, Nature shares the joy of their marriage because the union also fulfills and epitomizes the harmony of Creation. Similarly Nature's response at the Fall reveals how fully her concord depends upon the obedience of the human couple. And if Nature's compassion impresses upon us the lost harmony of Eden, the attribution of verbal power in manifesting those feelings reveals the clarity and familiarity with which Adam surveys a world the Fall will render obscure and alien.

Yet just as words ultimately fail to express the reality of God, so Nature is similarly limited. Following Hooker, Anglicans are disposed to accept a natural theology, and likewise one of the justifications provided for the scientific movement is that through knowing Nature we can know God. The more rigorous Protestant position, however, is skeptical of the powers of un-aided human reason, and it is therefore more reluctant to accept revelation in Nature as the means to achieve saving knowledge. Calvin contends that although God's revelation through his works was complete at Creation and remains constant, the fallen human being is unable to draw from it conclusions adequate for redemption. We can discern God in Nature correctly only through the clarifying agency of the written and spoken Word. Commenting upon Pentecost, he observes, "by faith it is understood that the worlds were ordained by the Word of God. (Heb. xi.3.) But faith is not conceived by the bare beholding of the heaven and earth, but by the hearing of the word. Whereupon it followeth, that men are brought by the direction of the word alone unto that knowledge of Almighty God which bringeth salvation."[14] Not even God's visions and miracles are efficacious without an explanation of their meaning: "Whenever God gave a sign to the holy patriarchs it was inseparably linked to doctrine, without which our senses would have been stunned in looking at the bare sign."[15]

Milton adopts Calvin's position and extends it, holding in the first place that Nature falls along with Adam and Eve. Thus "the Book of Knowledge fair" (III.47) is obscured both objectively, with reference to the perceived sign, and subjectively, with reference to the perceiver. And he further indicates that even in Eden the signs of God in Nature are insufficient without supplementary revelation. Although like the human couple Nature can declare his power and acknowledge his gifts, it cannot communicate directly God's "goodness beyond thought" (V.159). As Milton shows that the expressiveness of Edenic speech requires a poetic rather than a philosophic language, so he demonstrates the limitations of verbal and natural signs to communicate to Adam and Eve all they need to know about themselves and their relationship to God. Yet as they discover these limitations, the human couple grows in self-knowledge, which leads in turn to the knowledge of God that the external world cannot by itself supply, and so through the verbal process of questioning they acquire not simply information but the means of seeking their Creator that alone makes the indications of his presence significant to people.

[III]

Rationalist philosophers attributed to Adam, and hoped to recover through the exercise of reason, a language that communicates the essence of things immediately. But in expecting of words a function they cannot perform, these linguists at the same time sought to expunge from language its most characteristic resources, for they desired to make words completely transparent, circumventing the verbal process that speaks to a mind accustomed, as Raphael points out, to learning discursively rather than intuitively (V.488-490). Milton on the other hand, though he emphasizes with Augustine and most Reformation theologians the limited capacity of signs to convey the reality of God, also makes clear that if words are not sufficient to their referents, they are nonetheless the divinely sanctioned means by which we approximate the object.

In Augustinian/Calvinist epistemology, words like phenomenal signs convey knowledge in one of two ways: either they are indicative, pointing to a reality not yet known, or they are commemorative, evoking a prior experience.[16] Thus while words do not convey reality immediately, they can point to or evoke experience which verifies the aptitude of the sign. For theologians and religious poets, God is the ultimate goal of the quest for knowledge, and he is communicated through signs both indicatively and commemoratively. God reveals himself in Creation and in Scripture as parallel ways of accommodating himself to limited human powers of perception, and these external revelations are in part indicative, leading people to an ever fuller experience of their Creator. Accommodation is in the first instance condescension: God initiates his revelation to humans through external signs. But if signs are always inadequate to their *significata*, the disparity is greatest when the reference is to God. Thus the corollary to condescension is reticence. Even the angels cannot know God in his essence, but only as he chooses to manifest himself. Similarly, people know of God no more than is useful, with the result that they are always seeking yet never (or only rarely, under special and transitory circumstances) achieving total harmony with their Creator. But as the signs point us to an ever greater knowledge of God, they also recall what we already know.

Even the fallen person has, from birth, the same "sense of divinity" that leads Adam initially to infer a Creator from the Creation.[17] Through the action of grace, this intuition is reinforced by Christ, the Interior Teacher, who confirms from within the reality to which the external signs of God point. For Calvin as for Augustine, this operation of the indwelling Word is the crucial aspect of all learning. Edward Dowey has examined Calvin's application of this concept to Scriptural revelation: "True enough, the Bible has intrinsic validity. But this does not constitute its authority or even one source of its authority. The authority derives solely from the inner witness of God himself through which the intrinsic validity or inherent truth of the sacred oracles is recognized and confirmed."[18] But though they can never produce or create this internal confirmation, the external signs can lead us to a fuller consciousness of the Word within. Memory thus performs a central role in the acquisition of knowledge about God. This faculty is first engaged by the signs functioning commemoratively, evoking and in turn being confirmed by the Interior Teacher in a kind of dialectic between internal and external revelation. Further, subsequent knowledge of God subsumes yet never really transcends prior experience, and so education is cumulative, ever augmenting like Creation itself.

Although Adam's vision is clearer than that of his fallen progeny, his mind responds to signs in the same way as theirs. Following the meditative pattern Augustine employs, Adam perceives first the Creation, then himself, and this act of self-reflection leads him in turn to consider his Creator.[19] The first time he sees the sky, he springs erect "By quick instinctive motion" (VIII.259), intuitively distinguishing himself from the other animals in posture as his capacity to speak distinguishes him in constitution. His earliest recollections are of sensory experience, but he soon comes to reflect on himself, and he poses the ontological question, "But who I was, or where, or from what cause" (VIII.270) to a universe that cannot help him. Unlike Satan, who argues that he is "self-begot, self-rais'd" (V.860) because he is unable to recall an existence prior to

himself, Adam surveys the cosmos and acknowledges his own
contingency:

Ye Hills and Dales, ye Rivers, Woods, and Plains
And ye that live and move, fair Creatures, tell,
Tell, if ye saw, how came I thus, how here?
Not of myself; by some great Maker then,
In goodness and in power preëminent. (VIII.275-279)

But even though it is a sign of divinity, Nature cannot impart
direct knowledge of its referent. The authoritative response
Adam seeks comes only through revelation, but as his experience
with Nature leads him to question his own place in its scheme, so
the external voice of God or of his messenger Raphael imparts its
lessons by making them inseparable from Adam's growing consciousness of himself. Because, as Calvin remarks, God is within
people as well as external to them, "the knowledge of ourselves
not only arouses us to seek God, but also, as it were, leads us by
the hand to find him."[20]

If Adam's reading of the signs of God in Creation brings him
to acknowledge his contingency, so his verbal precocity leads
him to acknowledge the limitations upon his ability to rise above
the signs without divine aid. Where the fallen human being has
Scripture as the "spectacles" which allow a person to see correctly the signs of God in Creation, Adam enjoys direct revelation as the supplement to the Book of Nature.[21] Yet despite the
relative accessibility of God in Eden, Adam's powers of language
falter when he first meets his Creator, and thus in introducing
himself when Adam cannot find a suitable name, God extends
human language beyond its normal limitations. The lesson
about God, however, is inseparable from the self-knowledge the
incident engenders, for just as he cannot name Eve correctly
without also acknowledging his own identity, so his experience
with God's name leads him to understand more fully the nature
of their relationship. If, as God explains (VIII.343-345), the
naming of the animals seals Adam's lordship over the rest of
Creation, then his fruitless search for a name when he encounters God indicates his own subordination to the beings higher on
the Great Chain.

Adam's subsequent dialogue with his maker elaborates the role of verbal process in leading to greater self-knowledge and thus to the fuller knowledge of God. As the Logos appears to become increasingly conscious of the terms of his Sonship through the colloquy in Book III, so Adam gains Eve only when he is capable of articulating what his need for a mate signifies. God has condescended to speak with Adam in response to the queries he directs to Creation concerning the Creator, but in his reticence, withholding from Adam his intention to provide a mate, he allows Adam to discover for himself the differences between man and God.[22] In reply to God's feigned puzzlement at his discontent, Adam reminds him,

> Thou in thyself art perfet, and in thee
> Is no deficience found; not so is Man,
> But in degree, the cause of his desire
> By conversation with his like to help,
> Or solace his defects.   (VIII.415-419)

Providing the occasion for this process of self-discovery, God prepares Adam to accept Eve as a reminder of his own incompleteness, so that he will not fail to remember what Satan, arguing himself his own creator, willfully forgets.

Both Adam and Eve are intrinsically valuable, and their value is enhanced by the reciprocal love they share, yet each is also a sign to the other of his or her mate's identity. Because each needs the other to fulfill his or her own role, both are aware of their incompletion as individuals. Raphael suggests the possibility that their relationship, as well as their appreciation of all Creation, may continue to develop without end:

> . . . Love refines
> The thoughts, and heart enlarges, hath his seat
> In Reason, and is judicious, is the scale
> By which to heav'nly Love thou may'st ascend,
> Not sunk in carnal pleasure, for which cause
> Among the Beasts no Mate for thee was found.
>
>   (VIII.589-594)

Thus the particularly human nature of Adam's need for a mate is a reminder of his human responsibility to exercise his reason, controlling his fascination with Eve and directing it to spiritual ends in a straightforward Neoplatonic progression from earthly to divine love. Eve, on the other hand, has Adam's more dignified presence to remind her of his sovereignty in this process of exaltation.

But their development is not as linear as Raphael's description of love's refinement suggests. The free and joyous play of the exploring unfallen mind must occasionally reach an educative cul-de-sac. Some critics have taken these Edenic false starts as an indication that Adam and Eve are fatally flawed from the outset. Certainly the reader, aware of the story, can detect in the couple characteristic tendencies which, when yielded to, will prove disastrous. But for Adam and Eve they are no more ominous than the tumble of the speaker in Marvell's "The Garden," whose most serious lapse is that "Ensnared with flowers, I fall on grass." The couple's experience with verbal and phenomenal signs allows them to grow in knowledge, but while pursuing this course they must necessarily probe less rewarding ways in order to be surer of the right one when they are led to discover it for themselves. They are as free to make false starts as they are to fall, but the former freedom, as it increases their knowledge of self and God, is actually a safeguard, though of course not an absolute bar, against the latter. In this way Milton avoids the problem of embarrassingly primitive innocence, on the one hand, and a static but dull completeness, on the other, in his depiction of unfallen humanity. What keeps their exploration within bounds is the persistent, tutoring voice of God and his agent Raphael, whose response to the propensity of the human mind to educate itself is to explicate the signs which are most crucial or most unyielding to human attempts to probe their mystery.

Typically, as with Adam's initial encounter with his Creator, this elucidating voice evokes self-reflection which ends in acknowledgment of human contingency and God's sovereignty. Once explained, the Tree of Knowledge becomes a reminder of Adam's subordination just as Eve is a reminder of his incompletion. These signs are explicated before he has the opportunity to deviate from the divine plan, to take their meaning amiss. But in his later experiences, and in Eve's, human development is manifested in pursuits which require divine direction. Eve's "narcissism" is the first of these incidents. Citing Peter Sterry as an authority, Lee Jacobus defends Eve's fascination with her own image as an attempt, laudable in aim if faulty in method, at self-knowledge.[23] If Jacobus is right, it seems further significant that it is a divine voice, a direct revelation, which leads her from an image inadequate to communicate her identity, and that the voice urges her with an apostrophe which describes the purpose of her creation: "Mother of human Race" (IV.475). But it is Adam, replacing the epithet with the synonymous name "Eve," who persuades her to accept the role and the subordination it entails. Though her reflection is attractive, Eve admits, her marriage has shown her "How beauty is excell'd by manly grace / And wisdom, which alone is truly fair" (IV.490-491).

To Raphael the lesson Eve offers here is one Adam seems in danger of forgetting. Though the process of articulating his need for a mate should define his response to her, in fact her person seems nearly as arresting to him as her image had been to the less well-informed Eve. His doting praise elicits from the angel a stern admonition to remember the hierarchy of values implicit in his narration of Eve's creation:

> . . . be not diffident
> Of Wisdom, she deserts thee not, if thou
> Dismiss not her, when most thou need'st her nigh,
> By attribúting overmuch to things
> Less excellent, as thou thyself perceiv'st.
>
> (VIII.562-566)

Adam responds, assuring Raphael that despite his confession he knows enough to "Approve the best, and follow what I approve" (VIII.611). And if subsequent events show him abandoning that pursuit, still there is no reason here to doubt Adam's steadfastness.

[IV]

The pressure that Adam's probing mind exerts in exploring the world about him, supplemented as it is with divine guidance, leads to knowledge. But each advance is premised on what has gone before, and typically every sign that functions indicatively, leading Adam to new experience, has also a commemorative dimension, evoking and enriching his prior discoveries about himself and God. Thus even when he is unable to resolve a problem that presents itself in external Nature, the attempt leads him to appreciate more fully his own place and his relationship to Creation and Creator. This is the case when, in his discussion with Raphael about astronomy, he infers worth not from beauty, as he has with Eve, but from size and luminosity. Raphael's gentle reproof serves to correct this tendency to oversimplify. Even though Adam's facility with signs and Raphael's superhuman knowledge both falter before the problem of the universe's precise shape, the angel's admonition to "be lowly wise" (VIII.173) is a positive lesson, for if it does not provide Adam with the answer he seeks, it nonetheless reminds him of the address to all the signs of God appropriate to the human mind, a review his doting on Eve shows he needs.

Even though Nature cannot communicate God directly, it can provide an important first step in acquiring knowledge of the Creator, as Adam's earliest recollected experience indicates. George Puttenham in fact makes poets the first priests because "forasmuch as they were the first that entended to the observation of nature and her works, and specially of the Celestiall courses . . . searching after the first mover . . . , they were the first that instituted sacrifices of placation, with invocations and worship."[24] The orisons and vespers of Adam and Eve reveal the worshipful attitude the contemplation of the heavens is capable of inspiring. Yet when Adam seeks to learn more about celestial movement than Raphael volunteers to tell him, the angel not only refuses to elaborate but denies the validity of the question. Because of the clear relationship of Adam's unfallen uxoriousness to his later sin, his false start regarding his identity and his mate's has been generally accepted as relevant to the drama of the poem, even when it has raised questions about Milton's doctrinal consistency. The discussion of astronomy, however, has drawn more serious criticism. Howard Schultz excuses it, noting that for the seventeenth century, "In contrast to self-knowledge, astronomy became a favorite symbol of idle curiosity."[25] In "Vanity (I)," for example, Herbert uses the astronomer's probing as an instance of man's distraction from God: "Poor man, thou searchest round / To find out death, but missest life at hand." But to an age which values disinterested scientific inquiry with fewer reservations, lowly wisdom sounds suspiciously like blissful ignorance. Arthur Lovejoy has urged the impropriety of the passage, objecting that the angel's equivocal reply to Adam reveals Milton's illiberalism to the poem's detriment:

> For the dialogue between Raphael and Adam, in so far as it relates to seventeenth-century astronomy, obviously had no natural place in an epic of the Fall of Man; it was not a part of the "plot" of the poem nor of the dramatic characterization of the human protagonist. The subject was violently introduced—"dragged in"—because Milton had in mind his contemporary readers and wished to bring them to accept a theorem of his own. . . .
>
> Milton's position, in short, is pragmatic, in the most vulgar sense of that ambiguous term, the sense in which it designated an obscurantist utilitarianism hostile to all disinterested intellectual curiosity and to all inquiry into unsolved problems about the physical world.[26]

In terms of Adam's education, however, the passage on astronomy is parallel to the dialogue about Eve. In both cases, Adam seems about to lose himself in external Creation when, properly regarded, all of Nature, including Eve, is a reminder of his own place in the divine scheme, and Raphael's purpose is less to circumscribe the range of human inquiry than to recall to Adam what sort of knowledge is most valuable and how it is acquired. Even for the fallen human being, knowledge begins with the senses. After the Fall, this epistemological prerequisite is fraught with danger, as Satan demonstrates when, in preferring Eden to Heaven, he chooses the corporeal sign over the spiritual reality to which it points. But for Adam, provided only that they are subject to restraint, the senses are a medium through whose transmission knowledge is virtually equated with pleasure. In conversation with the angel, Adam enjoys the sensuosity of the words as well as their meaning, hearing Raphael "With wonder, but delight" (VIII.11). Only in the rapture that attends direct revelation from God is Adam completely exempt from recourse to sensory perception, and he collapses as a result of the strain this kind of learning places on him:

> My earthly by his Heav'nly overpower'd,
> Which it had long stood under, strain'd to the highth
> In that celestial Colloquy sublime,
> As with an object that excels the sense,
> Dazzl'd and spent, sunk down, and sought repair.
>
> (VIII.453-457)

Adam's speculations about astronomy remove him from this important first source of knowledge without the warrant of ecstatic communion. Noting that the immense distances involved make certainty impossible, Raphael points out to Adam that he is proceeding on the basis of inadequate data:

> God to remove his ways from human sense,
> Plac'd Heav'n from Earth so far, that earthly sight,
> If it presume, might err in things too high,
> And no advantage gain. (VIII.119-122)

And despite Lovejoy's charges, Adam's overly hasty leap from a few observable phenomena to a theory that will save those appearances is a violation of the scientific methodology Milton is said to be scorning. If contemporary issues are at all relevant, the choice seems to be not so much between Ptolemy and Copernicus as between the empirical, Baconian method of inquiry and the speculative, Cartesian one. Raphael, speaking for Bacon as well as for Milton and God, seems to get the better of the argument.

But the issues of seventeenth-century science, while vital to history and no doubt engaging to Milton, are peripheral to the major current of the poem. What is significant is the belief Milton shares with Bacon, which is manifested in the latter's inductive methodology, that to humans truth is partial and is to be pieced together only gradually. Bacon's religious avowals notwithstanding, he is mainly concerned with the application of perception and reason in the realm of natural philosophy, and his mammoth projects give evidence that he believes humans capable of completing the puzzle. Milton's emphasis on human fallenness, on the other hand, makes him skeptical that the *novum organum* can be completed in any meaningful way prior to the Second Coming, and he addresses the Creation chiefly as a means to know God. Like Herbert, he draws the popular distinction between *scientia* and *sapientia*, knowledge of things and knowledge of truth, that is implicit in Augustine's similar attack on astronomers: "They can see an eclipse of the sun long before it happens, but cannot see their own eclipse when it is actually taking place. For they do not approach the matter in a religious spirit and ask what is the source of the intelligence which they use to inquire into all this."[27]

The intellectual leap Adam fails to negotiate here Eve will later attempt, but with disastrous results. Without Adam, her reminder of the limitations of being human, Eve accepts Satan's argument to taste the fruit. In effect, he convinces her on the one hand that it is just an apple, without significatory value, and on the other that it has magical properties which will allow her to bypass the process whereby the human ascends to the divine only by stages. Adam's fall is more damning, in part because he does it willfully, in part because he has Eve there as a tacit reminder that he should know better. But he ignores the truths about himself he had acknowledged when he requested a companion. They are both unfinished, in the process of attaining their potential, and hence they must accept the guidance of their Creator. Yet he takes Eve, as he has said earlier, to be "in herself complete" (VIII.548), and as a result he precipitates the poem's climactic episode.

Adam's fall, like Eve's, is partly an epistemological lapse. The delight Eve provides for Adam begins to overcome his reason, and he is limited at the Fall to the sensory and passionate faculties as he has been limited in the dialogue on astronomy to the purely intellectual. But as both Raphael and Eve demonstrate, the dualism which separates delight from reason and spirit is false. Earlier, Adam's precocity has led him to criticize Nature's apparent prodigality in apportioning the universe. It has, Adam observes, appointed bodies of greater magnitude "merely to officiate light / Round this opacous Earth" (VIII.22-23). Raphael's reply suggests that Adam's theories result from a twofold failing: his speculations separate intellectual from sensory pleasures, and he refers what he observes not to God but to himself. Adam's impatience with empiricism is an aspect of the former mistake, and Eve's departure anticipates the angel's judgment at a dramatic level. Eve, Milton tells us, is as capable of purely speculative discourse as Adam is, but she prefers to receive her lessons from her husband, who will "intermix / Grateful digressions, and solve high dispute / With conjugal Caresses" (VIII.54-56).

Adam's second failing follows from the first. As he is temporarily limited to his intellect in trying to dissect what he should simply appreciate, so he is unable to rise above reason to apprehend what intellect cannot fathom. He assumes that he is, like the human figure in da Vinci's squared circle, the measure of all things, or, at the very least, that his reason is sufficient to discover the precise nature of the universal scheme. But Raphael must provide him with a gloss on the Book of Nature more adequate than the one he is able to imagine. The angel approves Adam's inquisitiveness, but he makes clear that no value attaches to magnitude for its own sake: "Great / Or Bright infers not Excellence" (VIII.90-91). As phenomena, the heavenly bodies are important to people only insofar as they serve their lives, and as signs only as they lead the observer to God. Whatever their other purposes may be, Adam is in no position to detect them. Viewing the universe, people must admire its beauty, recognize their own contingency, and celebrate the Creator. In Raphael's words,

> And for the Heav'n's wide Circuit, let it speak
> The Maker's high magnificence, who built

So spacious, and his Line strecht out so far;
That Man may know he dwells not in his own;
An Edifice too large for him to fill,
Lodg'd in a small partition, and the rest
Ordain'd for uses to his Lord best known.

(VIII.100-106)

Raphael, then, does not place arbitrary limits on human inquiry. Rather, he reforms Adam's attitude toward inquiry. God's book communicates God, points to him, but the meaning cannot be grasped by any one faculty. For Milton as for Calvin, knowledge of God engages the whole personality, and Adam's address to Creation should approximate that of Erasmus's pious Epicurean, who advises,

> the godly man beholds with reverent, innocent eyes, and with surpassing inward delight, the works of his Lord and Father, marveling at every one, finding fault with none but giving thanks for all, since he considers them all to be created for man's sake. And so in individual things he reveres the Creator's omnipotence, wisdom, and goodness, of which he discerns traces in created objects.[28]

Thus Eve's withdrawing when Adam and Raphael begin to discuss astronomy is not Milton's way of belittling feminine mentality. Instead, it represents in dramatic terms the same lesson Raphael has tried to make clear: Creation is to be both enjoyed and understood as a sign of God; to examine it critically is to forget one's place in it.

But Raphael's reasons for advising Adam to "be lowly wise" leave Lovejoy skeptical. To him, the angel's ignorance or indifference at the answer to the question is another trick of Milton's arrogant God: "It is even suggested that the stellar system may have been so constructed as to be an insoluble enigma to astronomers in order that the Creator may chuckle over their blunders."[29] To one who approaches Creation in the attitude Raphael and Erasmus enjoin, however, Lovejoy's objection would not occur. Even though God is the referent for all inquiry, one should not expect that the process implies a goal that people

can reach. God condescends to people, revealing himself partially in Creation, and people are expected to answer this accommodating movement with spiritual striving. But the corollary to
condescension is reticence, which makes the process of exaltation
unending. Yet the process is pleasurable, offering rewards of
delight which are not separable from the goal the process contemplates. As the speaker in Donne's "Lovers' Infiniteness"
understands, the elusiveness of finality is the source not of
frustration but of an opportunity to be continually refreshed:
"Yet I would not have all yet, / He that hath all can have no
more, / And since my love doth every day admit / New growth,
thou shouldst have new rewards in store." Creation like Eve
provides Adam with "ever new delight" (V.19).

Lovejoy's use of the term "enigma" is revealing in this context. Paul's description of our seeing God as "through a glass,
darkly" (*per speculum in aenigmate*; I Cor. 13:12) recalls from
Ciceronian rhetoric the concept of *aenigma*, which Augustine
defines as "a similitude . . . that is obscure and hard to discern."[30] In this rhetorical figure he finds an appropriate means of
discussing God because the difficulty of the language calls attention to the transcendent nature of the referent. But metaphoric
language can also be effective even where discursive language is
adequate. Discussing a passage from Canticles that he has just
allegorized, Augustine admits,

> But why it seems sweeter to me than if no such similitude
> were offered in the divine books, since the thing perceived is
> the same, is difficult to say and is a problem for another
> discussion. For the present, however, no one doubts that
> things are perceived more readily through similitudes and
> that what is sought with difficulty is discovered with more
> pleasure.[31]

Extrapolating from Scripture to the Book of Nature, Adam's
only text, we can recognize that the cosmic enigma that annoys
Lovejoy is really presented as an opportunity for growth and
pleasure. The simile is a recurrent technique for Milton, who
uses it often as a way to indicate the ineffable. The device is one
of overtopping, leading us from a reality with which we are

familiar to one for which our world is only a shadowy type. To
accommodate his readers, whose medium is more fully time than
space, Milton draws his examples from history. But Adam has
no history in this sense, and so Raphael uses space as the
narrator uses time. Adam's problem with astronomy, then,
functions as a cosmic epic simile, carrying Adam from his
relatively simple theory to a reality beyond the capacity of even
unfallen ratiocination. In his precocity he offers a Ptolemaic
model, only to have Raphael suggest the more elaborate Coper-
nican theory and finally to offer a further complication, the
possibility of multiple creations. Given this progress toward an *O
altitudo*, Adam's subsequent humility is both appropriate to piety
and intellectually responsible.

Through Raphael's discourse on astronomy, Adam brings to
fuller consciousness what his "birth" and education have already taught him about himself and his Creator. Despite his
intellectual clarity and the expressive powers of his speech,
Nature cannot disclose and the human mind cannot grasp the
extent of God's beneficence, but the effect of discovering these
limitations for himself is to stimulate Adam's powers of reflection. Thus even as the external signs of God, supplemented with
divine or angelic glosses, lead him toward an illumination ever
more complete, they also bring him to a self-knowledge that is
inseparable from the knowledge of God within. But for Adam as
for fallen human beings the quest for full understanding is
impossible to achieve, either through reason or through the
exclusive guidance of the Interior Teacher. Rather the dialectic
between external and internal revelation, between the signs that
point to God above and the sense of contingency that leads us
finally to attend more fully to the inner Word, is a never-ending
process. Although human words are inadequate especially when
their referent is divine, they perform an indispensable function in
bringing people to a knowledge of God, a knowledge whose
perpetual imperfection offers the opportunity for the joy of
unending discovery.

CHAPTER TWO

"Barbarous Dissonance"

~❧~

The Epic War of Words

IN his presentation of unfallen language, Milton offers metaphor and pun where the linguists expect mathematical precision, opulent redundancy where they imagine terseness. Employing this verbal play, Adam and Eve are able to express their thoughts immediately and fully, and their words identify their referents without becoming a substitute for them. Through Raphael the couple acquires a fuller understanding of the relationship of verbal and natural signs to the objects they are meant to convey, but the angel's mission is not simply to demonstrate the way Edenic speech works. Rather he is to provide the human couple with knowledge sufficient to resist Satan's duplicity. For while Milton does not accept the prevailing notion of language before the Fall, he does join with his contemporaries in finding a close association between verbal and moral lapses. Like the minister Robert South, a favorite of Charles II, Milton perceives verbal deception, deliberate misnaming, at the root of Original Sin: "God commanded, and *told Man what was Good*, but the Devil sur-named it *Evil*, and thereby baffled the Command, turned the World topsyturvy, and brought a new Chaos upon the whole Creation."[1]

Milton's epic voice begins his story of human disobedience in Hell because, through the impairment of intellect suffered at the Fall, his readers can know good only in contrast to its opposite. For Adam and Eve, of course, evil is not instrumental to the

knowledge of good, but to prepare them as fully as possible for
their encounter with Satan, Raphael must not only warn them
that the threat exists and that the assault will occur "by deceit
and lies" (V.243). He must also find the means to demonstrate
how false language operates and how its effects may be resisted.
In order to execute this aspect of God's charge, the angel
narrates the story of Satan's rebellion. Critical discussions of the
war in heaven generally focus either on the sources, gauging the
resonances with biblical and classical texts, or on the way the
reader is expected to evaluate Raphael's disclaimers and narrative inconsistencies.[2] But these approaches, while they address
issues important to our full understanding of the passage, tend to
slight the fact that Raphael's audience is Adam and Eve, whose
experience provides them with no means of detecting literary
echoes, no basis for judging the verisimilitude of the account. If,
as Arnold Stein argues, laughter is the appropriate response to
Satan's pretensions, then Adam, lacking a false sense of the
heroic to be purged, seems to prove himself an unfit audience.[3]
Moved instead to astonishment, he forces us to consider once
more the relationship of the events Raphael describes not only to
our own world but to Eden: "Great things, and full of wonder in
our ears, / Far differing from this World, thou hast reveal'd"
(VII.70-71).

     Although the narrative inevitably engages knowledge Mil-
ton's fallen readers bring with them to the poem, the relevance of
that knowledge can be assessed only if we allow our perspective
to be divided. As Adam and Eve must from their Edenic prospect try to apprehend "things so high and strange" (VII.53), so
we from our fallen viewpoint must approximate both heavenly
and innocent perception without forgetting the circumstances
which make complete understanding impossible. Once we appreciate the significance of the narrative to Raphael's primary
auditors, we can more accurately determine its place in the
poem. Adam and Eve need most to know not just the destruc-
tiveness of evil or the certainty with which it is punished, but the
virtuous guises it is capable of assuming. Only if they are
sufficiently apprised of the means Satan will employ to subvert
their happiness can the temptation be a genuinely decisive test of

their obedience. Our experience, then, converges with Adam and Eve's on the basis of what the narrative reveals: however the conflict may be expressed, its most important feature is its dramatization of the fall of language. And as they can hope to preserve their innocence only by knowing the ways of their enemy, so we can recognize the terms on which language must be redeemed only if we first appreciate the nature of its corruption.

[I]

For Milton's readers the ambiguity of words, their capacity to deceive and manipulate, is a condition fundamental to their experience. Hell, the world through which we enter the poem, is terrain all too familiar to the postlapsarian mind, and the frequency with which we are disillusioned leads us to recognize in the exposure of Satan's rhetoric and spectacle a common if perpetually chastening experience.[4] To the reader, then, Raphael's narrative of the origins of duplicity functions commemoratively, serving to clarify what our experience has already taught us. But the assumptions the account forces us to bring to full awareness Adam acquires only through the offices of Michael, the patient remedial teacher of the last books. Raphael must therefore introduce the human couple to the possibility of conscious deception by relying exclusively on the indicative force of words. Even though Adam and Eve have as yet no direct experience of a reality which Raphael can evoke the memory of, he can acquaint them vicariously with corrupt speech in the same way that Eve in her dream can confront evil without being subject to its taint.

The ability to interrupt and divert the spontaneous flow from thought to its disclosure is a Satanic invention that enters the poem's chronology at the moment of his revolt, and if he begins his career as a rebel by concealing his intentions, he further violates the linguistic standards of Eden by questioning the applicability of words to their referents. Lying requires deliberation, for the speaker must recognize that what is said is different from what is known. Thus Satan's calculated secrecy creates the circumstances necessary for deception to occur, but while he inspires the first lie, he does not speak it. Instead he enlists the aid of a lieutenant, who transmits his orders faithfully although he is aware that the stated purpose of assembling Satan's forces is not the real one (V.694-704). Like his demonic muse, then, the officer begins to use words more for their effect than for their ability to reveal the self. And as he has rendered the expressive power of words problematic, so Satan also casts doubt upon their referential value. Echoing God at the exaltation (V. 600-601), Satan addresses his followers by their titles, but he immediately suggests that the ranks the titles designate may no longer apply, that the Son's ascendancy may have made their degrees hollow, "merely titular" (V.774). Later, trying to represent the war as a genuine conflict, he mocks God's title as arbitrary: he invites Abdiel to "join him nam'd *Almighty* to thy aid" (VI.294). Where Adam's experience with the name of God serves to remind him of his own contingency, Satan's questioning of the title's rectitude here, like his subsequent application to God of inappropriate names, is an attempt to deny God's authority and thus to legitimize his rebellion.

By assuming the proposition that words and their referents have no necessary connection, Satan establishes the basis for recasting language to suit his purposes. When it is first introduced, for instance, the strategy allows Satan to make the concepts of freedom and kingship seem at odds by speaking of both in terms of a narrow definition of equality. He denies the legitimacy of the Son's exaltation because he cannot "in reason then or right assume / Monarchy over such as live by right / His equals, if in power and splendor less, / In freedom equal" (V.794-797). Dismissing in a dependent clause the ways in which the Son is superior, he leaves us to infer that as in unfallen speech the syntactical subordination reflects a scale of values in the nature of the referent. Thus we are invited to conclude that the equality of the Son and the angels, if true, is what is significant, and consequently that by making the Son monarch God defies reality and impairs the freedom of the others.

Manipulating diction and syntax, Satan practices a verbal magic which works on all his followers except Abdiel, whose steadfastness is due at least in part to his adherence to an unfallen linguistic standard. Not only does he resist Satan's rhetoric, but Abdiel detects in Satan the alteration which costs him his heavenly name even before God seals the loss with a curse. As the fallen angel has already begun to be disqualified for the name "Lucifer" and has not yet acquired a new one, Abdiel addresses him with epithets signifying the essential qualities of his character: "ingrate" (V.811), "Proud" (VI.131), "fool" (VI.135), "Apostate" (VI.172). Like Adam's naming the animals, Abdiel's perspicacity discloses both the nature of his opponent and his own continuing uprightness, a fact that Raphael's choice of epic similes, in a passage just prior to Abdiel's second confrontation with Satan, may be intended to emphasize. Describing the flight of the angels, Raphael reminds Adam of the time "when the total kind / Of Birds in orderly array on wing / Came summon'd over *Eden* to receive / Thir names of thee" (VI.73-76). Although the ostensible purpose of this comparison is simply to accommodate a heavenly event to Adam's experience, Milton's similes rarely confine themselves to their primary function. In this case the residual effect is to underscore for Adam the significance of the epithets Abdiel attaches to his foe.

While Abdiel's spiritual state is reflected in his verbal clarity, Satan's contribution to the flyting preliminaries continues and expands the ambiguity his earlier speech had initiated. As if uncertain how to handle this challenge to a skill not yet perfected, Satan uses no apostrophe in his first response to Abdiel and then resorts to an inversion much more crude than the complex blend of truth and falsehood with which he will exhort his followers in Hell or tempt Eve in the garden. Calling Abdiel "seditious Angel" (VI.152), the rebellious Satan implies that his position, the one from which Abdiel is dissenting, has as much claim to allegiance as God's.[5] His manipulation of words, then, is a function of his moral relativism. By subverting the belief that definitions can be constant, he hopes to induce his auditors to accept the language of the present moment as providing its own meaning. Luther defines the human word that is analogous to the divine as "not merely the utterance of the mouth . . . [but] the thought of the heart. Without this thought the external word is not spoken; or if it is spoken, it has substance only when the word of the mouth is in accord with the word of the heart. Only then is the external word meaningful; otherwise it is useless."[6] For Satan, on the other hand, words become merely counters, revealing neither the heart of the speaker nor any objective referent.

[II]

Satan's confrontation with Abdiel discloses the corruption language undergoes in the rebellion, but for Adam words are not the only means of expressing oneself. Appearance constitutes a language just as verbal signs do, and Satan is capable of obscuring its grammar as well. In unfallen creatures virtue is expressed in beauty and graceful action as it is in spontaneous eloquence. Milton emphasizes the correlation between inner state and exterior form by substituting moral abstractions for physical details in his description of Adam and Eve:

> Two of far nobler shape erect and tall,
> Godlike erect, with native Honor clad
> In naked Majesty seem'd Lords of all,
> And worthy seem'd, for in thir looks Divine
> The image of thir glorious Maker shone,
> Truth, Wisdom, Sanctitude severe and pure.
>
> (IV.288-293)

Assuming the reflection of spirit in matter, Adam greets Raphael as "Native of Heav'n, for other place / None can than Heav'n such glorious shape contain" (V.361-362). Likewise Raphael recognizes in Adam's speech and movement their divine origins: "for God on thee," he tells Adam, "Abundantly his gifts hath also pour'd / Inward and outward both, his image fair: / Speaking or mute all comeliness and grace / Attends thee, and each word, each motion forms" (VIII.219-223). Eve's beauty may tempt Adam to overvalue her, but it nonetheless reveals her genuine worthiness to be loved, and she at least acknowledges the superiority of "manly grace / And wisdom, which alone is truly fair" (IV.490-491).

The assumption that beauty reflects virtue is based upon the monistic ontology that is so apparent in Edenic experience. In the *Christian Doctrine* Milton declares, "spirit, being the more excellent substance, . . . contains within itself what is clearly the inferior substance; in the same way as the spiritual and rational faculty contains the corporeal, that is the sentient and vegetative faculty" (CPW, 6: 309). And the entire middle of the epic, from the beginning of Book V through the end of Book VIII, stresses repeatedly the continuity of spirit and matter. God's creation of the universe out of himself rather than *ex nihilo*, the accounts of angelic as well as Edenic lovemaking and digestion, and Raphael's promise that sustained obedience may lead to progressive refinement all point to matter as the medium for the revelation of spirit.

This quality of Paradise is all the more striking because it is so different from our experience of the fallen world. Satan of course cannot alter the nature of things, but he can affect our ability to perceive the continuity between spirit and matter that appears in Eden so straightforward. Thus while beauty is the true image of virtue, evil, as Uriel's failure to detect Satan's hypocrisy has demonstrated, can assume the form of its opposite without detection. Raphael describes the duplicity of Satan's appearance in lines Bentley took to contain a solecism: "His count'nance, as the Morning Star that guides / The starry flock, allur'd them, and with lies / Drew after him the third part of Heav'n's Host" (V.708-710). Bentley objected because "countenance" is the subject not only of "allured" but of "drew with lies," a possibility he found absurd: "He is the *Father of Lies* indeed, if not his Tongue, but his Countenance spoke them." Following one of Bentley's eighteenth-century respondents, however, Christopher Ricks shows that attributing to appearance the capacity to lie enriches our sense of Satan's methods.[7] Thus although Satan has devised syntactical ambiguity, Raphael converts it to the purpose of illumination rather than deception. And the lesson implied here is reinforced through the drama of Abdiel's encounter with Satan at the beginning of the war. While Abdiel has recognized verbal duplicity, he remains accustomed to drawing from beauty and power the same inferences that have led Adam to identify Raphael, and so he is shocked to find Satan still splendid despite his faithlessness:

> O Heav'n! that such resemblance of the Highest
> Should yet remain, where faith and realty
> Remain not; wherefore should not strength and might
> There fail where Virtue fails, or weakest prove
> Where boldest; though to sight unconquerable?
>
> (VI.114-118)

Like Abdiel, the human couple must realize that evil may appropriate the material as well as the verbal means created for the revelation of virtue, but the lesson Abdiel learns through experience, Adam and Eve must acquire vicariously. As narrator, then, Raphael faces a dual problem: he must convey to Adam and Eve the nature of a mind which operates in ways alien to their experience, and he must accomplish this task by tracing Satanic duplicity to its origins in an event beyond the power of human discourse to communicate, of human intellect to apprehend. He emphasizes his difficulty in the disclaimer with which he prefaces his narrative. Asking "how shall I relate / To human sense th'invisible exploits / Of warring Spirits" (V.564-566), he adopts the strategem of "lik'ning spiritual to corporal forms, / As may express them best" (V. 573-574). After having called the literal accuracy of his narrative into question, however, he qualifies the demurrer by suggesting "what if Earth / Be but the shadow of Heav'n, and things therein / Each to other like more than on Earth is thought?" (V.574-576). Ignoring the qualifier, William Riggs takes Raphael's diffidence as well as the narrative inconsistencies to be extensions of the humility the epic voice demonstrates in his invocations.[8] But while Raphael certainly joins Milton's narrator in stressing the limited capacity of human language to convey a divine subject, it is difficult to accept the implication in Riggs's reading that Milton seeks to illustrate the inadequacy of his medium by deliberately marring the coherence of Raphael's story. For Augustine it is the complexity of the language, not its inept handling, that reveals the difficulty of the subject; and to Milton the humility of the true servant lies not in doing badly what he could do better but in crediting God for whatever success his skill and dedication enjoy. As Herbert exclaims in "The Forerunners," "My God must have my best, even all I had." Thus Raphael's lapses in realism, what Samuel Johnson calls the "confusion of spirit and matter," must be interpreted not according to standards of warfare created by previous epics but in terms of their ability to mediate between the assumptions of Adam and Eve and what they need to know about fallen intellect.[9]

To the human couple, who cannot assess the verisimilitude of the narrative, the terms in which the battle is described work to reveal the way Satan renders problematic the relationship between spirit and matter, as between words and meanings, that obtains in Paradise. Using metaphors of verbal exchange to describe the battle, Raphael reveals that at the beginning of the war appearance and action serve straightforwardly to express their authors in Heaven as in Eden. When Abdiel accomplishes the transition from epic flyting to physical combat with the remark "This greeting on thy impious Crest receive" (VI.188), he is simply transferring terms from one medium of communication to another equally clear. Similarly the skirmish between Michael and Satan extends to action the hostilities begun verbally: "They ended parle, and both address'd for fight / Unspeakable" (VI.296-297). Further illustrating the continuity between spirit and matter, Michael's blow injures Satan's pride more deeply than it does his "Ethereal substance" (VI.330). He is borne on the shields of his followers back to his chariot, where "they him laid / Gnashing for anguish and despite and shame / To find himself not matchless, and his pride / Humbl'd by such rebuke, so far beneath / His confidence to equal God in power" (VI.339-343). The relationship between matter and spirit in the early part of Raphael's account is thus genuinely sacramental, and the terms in which he narrates the conflict reinforce what Adam's previous experience must lead him to believe: physical warfare is not simply a metaphor to accommodate, but a potentiation of, the spiritual discord that gives it rise. Although hostility itself is foreign to Adam, given its presence, he can readily suppose that it will manifest itself in action just as the spiritual love between himself and Eve reveals itself in sexual intercourse.

The language Raphael uses to describe the battle indicates the parallel function of word and action in Heaven: both express a precedent spiritual reality. But as Satan controverts the function of language, so he becomes increasingly adept at complicating the relationship between matter and spirit. Although his retention of heavenly beauty and power at the beginning of the confrontation seems un-self-conscious, he soon learns to manipulate appearance, using it to conceal the spiritual reality which it is ordained to manifest. Thus when accuracy requires the loyal angels to abandon metaphors which equate speech and action, Satan and his followers take them up. Like Raphael, Satan appropriates the language of rational dispute to describe his final escalation, but in his service the effect is reversed. Verbal similarity is used to obscure real difference, and as words assume priority over their referents, so matter becomes precedent to spirit. Introducing his ultimate weapon with "ambiguous words" (VI.568), Satan mocks the idea of reasoned debate by employing it as a vehicle for sheer force: "Heav'n witness thou anon, while we discharge / Freely our part: yee who appointed stand / Do as you have in charge, and briefly touch / What we propound, and loud that all may hear" (VI.564-567). And when the loyal angels are scattered, he taunts them in the same vein, inspiring Belial to similarly ponderous witticisms:

> Leader, the terms we sent were terms of weight,
> Of hard contents, and full of force urg'd home,
> Such as we might perceive amus'd them all,
> And stumbl'd many; who receives them right,
> Had need from head to foot well understand;
> Not understood, this gift they have besides;
> They show us when our foes walk not upright.

(VI.621-627)

Discussing this passage, Walter Savage Landor remarks, "It appears then on record that the first overt crime of the refractory angels was *punning*: they fell rapidly after that."[10] Although

Landor meant his observation only as a clever disparagement, he is correct to find in their puns an index to the angel's fallenness. Like his military formation, Satan's words work not to reveal but to obscure his intentions until the loyal troops are fully exposed.

Unlike Edenic wordplay, demonic puns are intended both to mock and to deceive, and Satan's rhetoric is adopted for its calculated effect on his hearers. Yet the result of using words to obscure things is to create a verbal reality capable of deluding even its authors. The extent to which Satan becomes the victim of his own deception is problematic, but if inspired words are the means to vision, then Satan by adopting a falsified language may indeed have denied himself access to truth. The effect of his attempt to supplant God's reality with his words is clear when, considering repentance, he claims to be prevented by "that word / *Disdain*" (IV.81-82). And just as words become more important than things, so for the fallen angels the material expression of hostility becomes more important than the spiritual state it reflects. Robert West has pointed out that for Henry More, "the fall of angels and the fall of man were both essentially the decline of pre-existing souls into inferior vehicles."[11] To Milton of course the essence of creatures does not alter at the Fall, but in preferring inferior to superior, Satan like Adam finds himself limited by his choice. If human love according to Raphael "is the scale / By which to heav'nly Love thou may'st ascend" (VIII.591-592), then hate is the means for angelic substance to become "gross" (VI.661), and Satan and his followers are made to feel the consequences their pursuit of material warfare entails. The injury Satan first feels is mostly to his pride, but Nisroch's pain is apparently at least partly physical, and finally they are all "crush't in and bruis'd" (VI.656) by their armor as the hurled mountains reach their targets. They are similarly trapped by their materialism at the conclusion, for their investment in force finally induces the Son to accept trial by combat, "since by strength / They measure all, of other excellence / Not emulous, nor care who them excels" (VI.820-822). As Belial's puns reveal, to the fallen angels matter has assumed priority over spirit, force like beauty becoming not a function of virtue but an attempt to compensate for its absence.

Although they recognize the perfidy of Satan's devices, the loyal angels can no more defeat him than the rebels can actually shake the throne of God. Because the forces are so evenly matched, the war is a stalemate, promising only infinite escalation if left to the combatants to resolve. The absence of resolution may lead us to redefine heroism, seeing it as "standing only," the energetic commitment to doing God's work without any illusion that the success of the undertaking depends upon the effort of his creatures.[12] But it is also true that the loyal angels are impaired because military conflict is a Satanic medium.[13] Milton's narrator implies the triviality of conventional heroism when in the last invocation he finds epics of physical glory to evince only "The skill of Artifice or Office mean, / Not that which justly gives Heroic name / To Person or to Poem" (IX.39-41). And as the epic voice condemns the terms in which war is celebrated, God shows his impatience with the thing itself, dispatching the Son to end the angelic charade with the comment, "War wearied hath perform'd what War can do" (VI.695). While Abdiel has struck the first blow in the battle, and while certainly the loyal angels are not degraded by participating in an activity which God has sanctioned, nonetheless the war they conduct has Satan as its author. Thus like their rebel counterparts the unfallen angels don armor, and though they are not injured, their natural freedom is restricted. The advantage Satan holds here is similar to the one he enjoys in debate: he cannot lose once he is allowed to define the terms of the contest.

Unable to vanquish Satan's forces, the good angels defer willingly to the Son, whose power raises the conflict to another plane. Instructed perhaps by God's irony, he devalues warfare even as he participates in it. For while he appears in military splendor to execute God's declaration of war, he never enters lists with his foes. Rather, he defeats them simply by his presence. As the landscape mends itself in response to his passing, so the fallen angels are enervated by the penetrating eyes of his chariot, "that wither'd all thir strength, / And of thir wonted vigor left them drain'd, / Exhausted, spiritless, afflicted, fall'n" (VI.850-852). Confronted by the Word, the source of their derived power, they lose the energy with which Satan's false words have infused their rebellion, and consequently, although the Son intends to "root them out of Heav'n" (VI.855), they remove themselves voluntarily, preferring the abyss to his pursuit. To Adam and Eve the victory of the Word must suggest that, while lesser beings may not be able to defeat Satan decisively, the power of truth will prevail in time over the strategies of deception. And if Raphael's explicit warnings about duplicity as a Satanic weapon are relatively few, the narrative itself makes a clear impression on the human couple. From Adam's reluctance to let her work apart, Eve correctly infers his suspicion that Satan will tempt her with lies: "His fraud is then thy fear" (IX.285). Once she makes the issue explicit, Adam alludes to Raphael's account to justify his concern: "Subtle he needs must be, who could seduce / Angels" (IX.307-308); and his final warning reiterates the lesson only the story of Satan's rebellion could have taught him: "Reason not impossibly may meet / Some specious object by the Foe suborn'd, / And fall into deception unaware, / Not keeping strictest watch" (IX.360-363).

[III]

Through narrating the story of the war in heaven, Raphael illustrates to Adam and Eve the duplicity Satan will employ to effect their fall. But events that strike the innocent mind as strange and wondrous are integral to the experience of Milton's contemporaries. To religious reformers in particular, military conflict provided a ready source of comparisons with which to emphasize the urgency and strenuousness of the struggle between good and evil. Calvin cautions, "It is the will of the Lord . . . that his Church shall be engaged in uninterrupted war in this world. That we may continue to be his disciples to the end, it is not enough that we are merely submissive, and allow ourselves to be governed by his Word. Our faith which is constantly attacked by Satan, must be prepared to resist."[14] And as William Haller has shown, warfaring is along with pilgrimage one of the most common ways of describing the Christian life in seventeenth-century English sermons.[15] Some Protestants take

literally Paul's admonition to "Put on the whole armour of God"
(Eph. 6:11), but others interpret the passage figuratively, as an
indication of the seriousness of the threat and the need to trust in
God for protection. Thus while Adam and Eve find in physical
combat first the natural expression of a spiritual state and then
Satan's attempt to conceal meaning by submerging it in matter,
Milton's readers tend to see the war in part as a metaphor
describing the perpetual hostility between the servants of God
and those of Satan. Yet if we must make a special imaginative
effort in order to appreciate the significance of the account to
unfallen ears, nonetheless the reader's perspective intersects
with that of Adam and Eve on the basis of the chief threat Satan
poses. For Milton's contemporary audience as for the human
couple and the angelic combatants, the struggle between good
and evil is a contest between false prophets and true, between
deceiving manipulators of language and the agents of the Word.

   Luther attributes the special animosity the devil bears for him
to his ability to disseminate divine truth:

> I know full well that while it is the Spirit alone who accom-
> plishes everything, I would surely have never flushed a covey
> if the languages had not helped me and given me a sure and
> certain knowledge of Scripture. I too could have lived up-
> rightly and preached the truth in seclusion; but then I should
> have left undisturbed the pope, the sophists, and the whole
> anti-Christian regime. The devil does not respect my spirit
> as highly as he does my speech and pen when they deal with
> Scripture. For my spirit takes from him nothing but myself
> alone; but Holy Scripture and the languages leave him little
> room on earth, and wreak havoc in his kingdom.[16]

Later reformers similarly see ministers as the primary target of
and defense against Satan's lies. In his gloss on the battle
described in Revelation, a major source for Milton's imagery,
David Pareus finds there an account of the early Church's
struggle against a foe whose primary weapon is his verbal
subtlety. According to his interpretation, the war reveals how
"Satan drew by flaterie and lying promises many teachers from
seeking after heavenlie things," and the names the fallen angel is

called suggest as well his chief instrument for working evil. If "Satan" retains the legalistic connotations of "adversary," "devil" signifies a "slanderour or false accuser."[17] The English Puritan Thomas Taylor on the other hand interprets Revelation as a foreshadowing of contemporary events, but he likewise warns that Satan's "speciall malice is intended against godly Ministers," and that a fundamental strategem is either to interrupt the supply of the Word as "victual from the Christian souldier" or to convert it to his own use: "The Word of God, a principall weapon, he can easily turne in our owne hands against our selves."

In charging Abdiel with treason and in meeting his loyalty with scorn, Satan resorts to ploys Taylor finds typical of his reaction to witnessing Christians. Exhorting his readers "to contend for the faith," he warns that "the dragon will call it faction, & turbulence, and daunt men with noyse of troublesome make-bates, as truly as *Eliah* was accused to trouble all Israell, when he destroyed the Altars of Baal." "What good he can neither hinder nor thus blemish," Taylor continues, "he will openly disgrace and revile: for he rageth against goodnesse, so that he never ceaseth to cast false and scandalous reproches and imputations against it."[18] Bunyan's preacher-combatant Great-Heart personifies the ideal response to Satan's calumny. Similarly Milton, answering the call to arms, frequently directs in his prose a "rhetoric of warfare" against opponents he regards as Satan's partisans.[19] In *The Second Defense*, for instance, he sees his pamphleteering as an activity parallel to soldiering and more appropriate to the defense of truth, and he wears his blindness as a war wound, having lost his sight while contending with his country's enemies (CPW, 4: 553, 588).

If the mortal nature of the struggle between good and evil makes the comparison with warfare seem apposite, however, Satan's own conduct casts him in the role not of honorable foe but of assassin and saboteur. Particularly after Guy Fawkes's failed attempt to assassinate King James with a bomb, preachers tended to find in the imagery of mining and explosives an especially fitting vehicle for describing treachery. In a sermon commemorating the fifth anniversary of the plot's failure, John

Rawlinson declares Fawkes and his cohorts more devious than Judas, "for *Judas* his policie wrought but above ground, but theirs wrought under ground: and the tooles of their treason were not *swords and staves* to apprehend, but *spades and pickaxes* to undermine."[20] Writing on Christ's temptation a few years after Rawlinson, Taylor alludes to the plot by way of attributing specifically to Satan the metaphoric tools of the saboteur. He gives Satan his due as a strategist, cautioning "never was there such an engineir so expert to winne and holde," and he later compares Satan's attempts to circumvent the Word to the secret warfare of the terrorist: "By fraud or secret Strategems, undermining the City of God, as the Powder Saints, and Salt-Petermen did the Parliament House."[21]

Milton, then, in depicting mining and the invention of explosives as acts of treachery, is drawing upon a common association in the seventeenth century. In his account, however, the fraudulence is specifically verbal, an identification suggested not only by the puns of Satan and Belial but also by the metaphor with which Raphael describes the devils' artillery. To him the cannons are false oracles: "thir mouths / With hideous orifice gap'd on us wide, / Portending hollow truce" (VI.576-578). But the connection is not solely Milton's. In his study of the influence of iconography on the imagery of *Paradise Lost*, Roland Frye calls attention to a fifteenth-century military manual and to a 1635 engraving by Callot, both of which represent cannon as dragons.[22] He correctly adduces these as evidence that artillery is commonly linked to demonic forces, but he fails to draw from these illustrations the further inference that Raphael's metaphor invites: the engines, their barrels represented as dragons' mouths, are symbols of the false prophecy and vilification the servants of God must withstand. As Raphael manages, in the lines to which Bentley objected, to convert the potentially Satanic ambiguity of syntax into a means for revealing Satan's character, here he transforms puns intended to obscure the devils' intentions into a metaphor which discloses their falsity.

For Augustine the failure to see beyond the literal to the figurative is an index of fallenness:

. . . you must be very careful lest you take figurative expressions literally. What the Apostle says pertains to this problem: "For the letter killeth, but the spirit quickeneth." That is, when that which is said figuratively is taken as though it were literal, it is understood carnally. Nor can anything more appropriately be called the death of the soul than that condition in which the thing which distinguishes us from beasts, which is the understanding, is subjected to the flesh in the pursuit of the letter. . . . There is a miserable servitude of the spirit in this habit of taking signs for things, so that one is not able to raise the eye of the mind above things that are corporal and created to drink in eternal light.[23]

Thus through Raphael's presentation we begin to see the cause for symptoms Milton's narrator has already revealed. For if the fallen angels begin in the war to limit their vision to the physical means of its conduct, we have already encountered in Hell the literalism and materialism that result. As Satan reduces the significance of the defeat to a matter of tactics, so Moloch addresses the question put before the assembly by denying a choice is possible. To him renewed assault is the inevitable result of the laws of physics:

> But perhaps
> The way seems difficult and steep to scale
> With upright wing against a higher foe.
> Let such bethink them, if the sleepy drench
> Of that forgetful Lake benumb not still,
> That in our proper motion we ascend
> Up to our native seat: descent and fall
> To us is adverse.   (II.70-77)

Ignoring the moral dimension of his words of direction, he reduces them strictly to their denotative meanings.

And if Moloch is in this speech a pure distillation of the literalism their fall has induced, so Mammon represents in concentrated form the materialism the devils have likewise adopted. Unlike the muse, who prefers "Before all Temples th'upright heart and pure" (I.18), Mammon seeks only external splendor: "ev'n in Heav'n his looks and thoughts / Were always downward bent, admiring more / The riches of Heav'n's pavement, trodd'n Gold, / Than aught divine or holy else enjoy'd / In vision beatific" (I.680-684). In Hell, however, gold is "precious bane" (I.692), suggesting that the term "trodd'n" is not just an adjective but a transitive verb: the value of the material is conferred by the creatures who use it and not by its intrinsic worth. Yet Mammon misses the subtlety of this point, and like the idolaters he inspires, he hopes to supplant God's "invisible / Glory" (I.369-370) with an image of his own creating:

> As he our darkness, cannot we his Light
> Imitate when we please? This Desert soil
> Wants not her hidden lustre, Gems and Gold;
> Nor want we skill or art, from whence to raise
> Magnificence; and what can Heav'n show more?
>
> (II.269-273)

Just as Mammon attempts to imitate heavenly splendor through physical opulence, so Satan seeks repeatedly to create in words a reality more congenial to his purposes than the one deriving from the Word. In order to justify his rebellion and his continued resistance, Satan must locate the source of God's authority in something other than nature. Thus he attributes God's victory to a military trick, making repugnant the thought that he could return to the service of a foe whose triumph was won so narrowly and deviously. Further, refusing "To bow and sue for grace / With suppliant knee, and deify his power" (I.111-112), he implies through the last verb that his vision like God's constitutes the reality it perceives. Having thus privately located God's power in the angels' worship of him, he later raises the issue publicly, wondering to his assembled retinue whether God reigns "upheld by old repute, / Consent or custom" (I.639-640). Yet his position is inconsistent, for while he speaks here as an iconoclast, he has first appealed to his troops as a conservative, interpreting the Son's begetting as an innovation which diminishes the privileges vested in their ranks. Similarly, in beginning the demonic council he proposes a war to regain their "just inheritance of old" (II.38), imputing to their previous status a legitimacy held apart from God's disposing and in which God does not share.

Posing in turn as a feudal lord and as an egalitarian in order to challenge God's authority, Satan creates a semantic vacuum of leadership and then agrees to fill it himself, enlarging his role from first among equals to monarch and finally to tyrant. He negotiates the former step simply by changing the subject of "reign" from the first person plural he employs in Book I to the singular of Book II:

> Wherefore do I assume
> These Royalties, and not refuse to Reign,
> Refusing to accept as great a share
> Of hazard as of honor, due alike
> To him who Reigns, and so much to him due
> Of hazard more, as he above the rest
> High honor'd sits? (II.450-456)

The second advance we note both from Milton's imagery and from Satan's actions. His throne is compared with that of an eastern king or sultan, the archetype of power arbitrarily exercised, and he manipulates his followers into approving a course of gratuitous cruelty as a diversion from the disastrous consequences of his leadership. Although he pledges to pursue "War / Open or understood" (I.661-662) at the bidding of his constituents, he has prearranged for the deliberations to sanction instead a campaign of desolation against creatures who have done the angels no injury and who are incapable of retaliating.

More than the pomp and the cruelty of Satan's reign, however, it is the instrument he uses to acquire and extend power that qualifies him as a tyrant. Milton's contemporaries held that false words exceed even military might as the despot's strongest ally. South warns of human susceptibility to the "bewitchery" of words: "There is hardly any Rank, Order, or Degree of Men, but more or less have been captivated, and enslaved by Words."[24] And in the sixteenth century Agrippa's description of the political abuses of eloquence might serve as a handbook for Satan's program: "For oftentimes men indewed with this arte do move conspiracie, and stirre sedition, whilest they with this artificial bablinge deceave some, backebite other, jeste at other, flatter other, and use a certaine tirannie against innocentes."[25] Nimrod, the first tyrant, was also according to tradition the architect of Babel, and commentators exploited the coincidence. Flavius Josephus, the Jewish scholar whose writings are the source of the tradition, finds Nimrod assembling his workers not through coercion but through sophistry:

> he put them in the head that they should not beleeve that their good hap proceeded from God, but that they ought to attribute it to their own vertue, which furnished them with so much riches: so that in a little space he reduced the estate to a tyrannie; supposing by this onely meanes that he might make men revolt against God, if he might perswade them to submit themselves to his government. . . . The common sort was ready to follow these ordinances of *Nemrod*, supposing it to be pusillanimitie in themselves, if they should obey God.[26]

If Nimrod was the first tyrant, he was also according to Luther the inventor of idolatry. The tower is "the false and deceitful church," and the chief result of the confusion of tongues is to increase "idolatry and superstition, since it made the ministry of the Word almost impossible."[27] But this role, too, reflects a desire to control others by manipulating their perception, for the splendor of things can become the visual counterpart to false rhetoric. Spectacle resembles Satanic language in creating an illusion of self-sufficiency, evoking a sense of wonder which transports the viewer. Invited to suspend the faculties of reason and judgment with which he normally assimilates new data to previous experience, the spectator thus becomes more susceptible to deceit. When Marlowe's Lucifer wants to divert Faustus's attention from the theological questions that perplex him, he presents a masque and urges his victim to "Talk not of

Paradise or creation, but mark the show."[28] In recognition of this danger, Jonson quarreled with Inigo Jones, the architect whose elaborate sets he felt were undermining the moral seriousness of his poetry. And Satan, exploiting the effect Jonson feared, enhances his power as did Charles I through pageant and visual opulence. For Mammon the archetypal idolater, the love of gold is an expression of his materialism, but to Satan the illusory splendor it creates can serve in tandem with his sophistry to divert his constituents from probing the contradictions of his claim to rule.

[IV]

The wiles Satan has invented in the war and refined in Hell he turns upon Eve with calamitous effect. His process of deliberation concludes with his choice of an appropriate disguise, and if he hopes the serpent's subtlety will lend credibility to the temptation, he has the additional advantage of the beast's dazzling beauty:

> . . . his Head
> Crested aloft, and Carbuncle his Eyes;
> With burnisht Neck of verdant Gold, erect
> Amidst his circling Spires, that on the grass
> Floated redundant: pleasing was his shape,
> And lovely . . .   (IX.499-504)

But though his appearance and behavior catch her eye, it is his ability to speak that arrests Eve's attention and elicits the fatal question: "Language of Man pronounc't / By Tongue of Brute, and human sense exprest? . . . Redouble then this miracle, and say, / How cam'st thou speakable of mute?" (IX.553-563). Despite what Raphael has taught, she too quickly infers reason from speech and thus becomes an accessory to her own undoing, assenting to Satan's detachment of words from their referents and then adopting his tactics as she presents the case to Adam.

Eve has first encountered Satan's sophistry in her dream. In the argument he presents there, he initially distinguishes between heavenly and earthly creatures and then invites her to join the angels as an equal, urging her to finish at once the process of exaltation with which, as Raphael points out, obedience is constantly being rewarded in Eden. But the act she intuitively resists in her dream Satan's more sophisticated approach will induce the waking Eve to perform. Extending the calculation which has led him to appropriate the serpent's form as a disguise, he converts his attraction to her beauty into a mask that will conceal his intentions: "Shee fair, divinely fair, fit Love for Gods, / Not terrible, though terror be in Love / And beauty, not approacht by stronger hate, / Hate stronger, under show of Love well feign'd, / The way which to her ruin now I tend" (IX.489 - 493). The metamorphosis of "Love" from a response to beauty into a Satanic disguise is accomplished by first reversing the negation "Not terrible," then supplanting "fair" with "terror," and finally interposing "hate" twice in positions successively more emphatic. Achieving a grammatical subordination of "Love," Satan in the process severs the word from its original reference to the feelings Eve engenders and makes it simply a self-generated role.

Having overcome through an act of will the disarming effect of Eve's beauty, Satan can then beguile her, leading her gradually from the world she knows and into one that exists solely in his words. At the beginning of the temptation, he uses a succession of apostrophes that moves from the literally accurate (for the serpent) but potentially ambiguous "sovran Mistress" (IX.532) through a series of titles that ascend in flattery as they descend in rectitude. If we begin to question the propriety of "sole Wonder" (IX.533), the next epithet "Fairest resemblance of thy Maker fair" (IX.538) makes the direction clear: he is elevating her above Adam, urging her to forget her marital obligations. And the drift of the literally correct but somehow suspicious use of "fair," applying the positive to God and the superlative to Eve, is realized at the tentative conclusion, which places Eve first "A Goddess among Gods" (IX.547) and then superior to them, commanding an obeisance from angels that they owe only to the deity. With regard to the fruit, Satan obscures its function as a sign of human contingency by calling it simply an apple (IX.585), and then, once it is linguistically divorced from its intended purpose, he imputes to it magic properties possessed apart from God's disposition (IX.602-612). Reinforcing his claim, Satan introduces doubt at the force of the proscription by converting a tautology, God is God, into a negative *gradatio*: "God therefore cannot hurt ye, and be just; / Not just, not God; not fear'd then, nor obey'd" (IX.700-701). And finally he redefines death, removing the dreadful connotations Eve has learned to associate with it and supplying her with new ones: "So ye shall die perhaps, by putting off / Human, to put on Gods, death to be wisht, / Though threat'n'd, which no worse than this can bring" (IX.713-715).

Satan's primary method of persuasion is thus to redefine concepts, making them amenable to more convenient interpretation, but he increases his chance of success by employing the rhetorical device of repetition. In his attack on a prescribed liturgy, Milton observes of repeated formulae, "As for the words, it is more to be fear'd lest the same continually should make them carelesse or sleepie, then that variety on the same knowne Subject should distract; . . . if men should ever bee thumming the drone of one plaine Song, it would bee a dull Opiat to the most wakefull attention" (*Anim*; CPW, 1: 691). The effect of Satan's repetitions, then, recalls Comus's description of the singing of his mother and the Sirens: "they in pleasing slumber lull'd the sense, / And in sweet madness robb'd it of itself" (260-261); and its purpose is to induce the forgetfulness Comus's potion causes.

To Augustine memory is an especially crucial faculty. As Adam's cumulative education shows, without the power to bring the past to bear on the present, we could not learn, for words would be simply disconnected sounds, sentences only unrelated syllables. And because experience is meaningful only when it is provided with an interpretive context, memory is essential as well to morality.[29] Thus while Comus's elixir owes its transforming power to the intemperance of those who indulge in it, their failure of will results in and is sustained by a failure of memory.

Like the crewmen of Odysseus who fall victim to Circe's spell, Comus's rout "Not once perceive their foul disfigurement, / But boast themselves more comely than before, / And all their friends and native home forget, / To roll with pleasure in a sensual sty" (74-77). Forgetting the restraints of their previous lives, they accept the standard of the present moment as an adequate guide, and the result is to perpetuate the degradation they have already suffered. Similarly, in order to believe Satan's argument, Eve must forget what she knows from past experience, preferring instead of that reality the illusory present Satan's words create.

Repetition then aims to accomplish through its insinuating, soporific effect the same suspension of critical faculties that spectacle and heroic eloquence achieve through wonder. But a part of the punishment of the fallen angels is never to drink the Lethean waters that will allow them to forget what they have lost, and thus despite Satan's growing sophistication in misusing language, insofar as he deals with reality he must confront the inability of his rhetoric to alter it. Although he has earlier insisted "The mind is its own place, and in itself / Can make a Heav'n of Hell, a Hell of Heav'n" (I.254-255), he must acknowledge as he surveys Eden that the localized Hell is Heaven only when compared to the spiritual torment he suffers:

> Which way I fly is Hell; myself am Hell;
> And in the lowest deep a lower deep
> Still threat'ning to devour me opens wide,
> To which the Hell I suffer seems a Heav'n.
>
> (IV.75-78)

The intrusive power of truth leads here to articulate confession, but later encounters render him silent or ineffectual in speech. While the unsuspecting Uriel is unable to distinguish Satanic duplicity from angelic zeal, Ithuriel and Zephon are more successful because they have been alerted to the danger. Thus the touch of Ithuriel's spear, which results in Satan's unintentional self-exposure, is the physical analogue to Zephon's penetrating scorn, whose effect is to leave Satan momentarily "abasht"

(IV.846). And because in Eden beauty is a reflection of virtue, he becomes for a moment "Stupidly good" (IX.465), paralyzed in stammering soliloquy as he spies on Eve's innocence. The effect of truth on Satan looks back to the chill the Lady strikes in the heart of Comus, and forward to the curiously diminished Adversary of the Word in *Paradise Regained*. But it also recapitulates the Son's victory in the war in heaven, where not his strength but only his presence is required to vanquish the rebels.

And if truth is capable of breaching even Satan's defenses, so it is always available as the means for his potential victims to resist the most seductive of his temptations. To its opponents in the sixteenth and seventeenth centuries, the force of rhetoric threatens to prove irresistible, but for Milton evil can always ultimately be detected despite the energies invested in its concealment. He consistently finds the logic of his religious and political opponents faulty, and he frequently notes that their style reflects their characters. Just as he is convinced that the virtue of the good poet will transform his art, so he believes that under careful scrutiny the language of false speakers will betray the corruption of its users. The Confuter in the Smectymnuan controversy reveals his shallowness through his "coy flurting stile . . . frumps and curtall gibes," and his short sentences (*Smec*; CPW, 1: 873); the anonymous respondent to *The Doctrine and Discipline of Divorce* becomes ridiculous for pretending to a knowledge of Greek and Hebrew while his usage, according to Milton, is illiterate (*Col*; CPW, 2: 724); and Salmasius stands condemned for "his foolish professorial talk" (*1st Def*; CPW, 4: 307) as well as for his position. Satan can certainly deceive those such as Uriel who have no reason to doubt his stated motives and who are not themselves being recruited to perform misdeeds. But Abdiel's loyalty, like the Lady's resistance of Comus and Gabriel's incisive logic, illustrates that despite the technical virtuosity Satan's rhetoric displays, the temptation to evil is not overpowering, and so Eve, forewarned by Raphael and Adam, is without excuse.

Satan cannot force words to submit entirely to his will because he is using a medium not of his own devising. If repetition in his service can have a mesmerizing effect, nonetheless the words whose definitions he attempts to subvert must inevitably function commemoratively, recalling the meanings which the poem confers upon them. We do not accept Moloch's reduction of words of rising and falling to their literal significance because the narrator has created a kind of linguistic firmament against which to measure fallen speech. The spatial adjectives have been imbued with moral connotations from the beginning of the poem, and they continue to color the terms of direction, undercutting Moloch's assertions even as he formulates them. Similarly the splendor of Pandemonium is deflated by contrast with the inward temple the muse prefers. Thus despite his attempt at redefinition, Satan's words must evoke a controlling context of divine and angelic language which Eve ignores only through an act of will.

From Raphael's account Adam and Eve have learned not only that signs can be manipulated for evil purposes but also how to deal with the resulting ambiguity. Words must be measured against their referents, appearance against reality as Abdiel does. But even then the resolution may not be final. As the loyal angels fight at best to a stalemate with the rebels, so human reason may not be able to vanquish Satanic duplicity even though it can expose its fraudulence. Fortunately, reason is not the last line of truth's defense. The Word, in heaven or in history, alone wields the power to dismiss the claims of Satan. But in the same way that the loyal angels must resist obediently until help arrives, humans must be able to withstand temptation, remaining steadfast despite the apparent might of the adversary while trusting God's power to resolve issues beyond the capacity of human resources. Disarmed by his serpentine flattery, Eve fails to examine carefully Satan's arguments, while Adam, confronted with what appears to be the eminent loss of his "heart's desire" (VIII.451), fails to refer to God a situation that seems beyond hope. Thus in their fall they reject what Raphael and their previous experiences have taught them, and as they yield to Satan's will, they also appropriate his use of language. They become calculating, they prefer lesser to greater goods, and as a result they introduce into human discourse the tension between words and meanings that has up to now been the sole property of demons.

In Genesis language is not explicitly cursed until the Babel episode, but many commentators trace the fall of language back to Eden. The German mystic Jacob Boehme, for instance, makes the verbal fall simultaneous with the violation of the divine command. Punishing the builders of Babel with the confusion of tongues, God according to Boehme simply manifests in form the legacy of social discord and intellectual degeneration Adam's sin had created in substance.[30] Richard Allestree extends the point still further, interpreting Genesis to imply that the corruption of speech is not simply the immediate consequence of the Fall but its essence: "Original sin came first out of the mouth by speaking, before it entred in by eating."[31] Similarly in *Paradise Lost* it is difficult to locate the Fall simply in the first bite Adam and Eve take of the fruit. If their sinful act makes the defiance of God's proscription irreversible, their decision to disobey is the result of adopting a corrupt rhetoric in order to justify their sin. As he tempts Eve, Satan at the same time teaches her to practice self-deception. Once she learns the lesson, she conveys it along with the fruit to Adam, who falls not because he accepts Eve's arguments but because he persuades himself that he cannot live without her.

Both Adam and Eve initiate their sin by soliloquizing, an act betraying a divided consciousness previously unknown to them, and if Adam cannot quite persuade himself that the curse on the fruit has been lifted, Eve seems genuinely convinced that her own reinterpretation is correct. The tree, she argues, is not a sign of their contingency but the avenue to divinity forbidden only because God fears their advance, and the threat of death is idle because it has not claimed the serpent. And in accepting Satan's arguments, she also begins to imitate his rhetoric. Before eating the fruit she praises the tree for its gift of "elocution" (IX.748), but as Anne Ferry observes, she no longer conceives of this power in terms of Edenic language: "By 'elocution' she means speech, but the redundancy of the first two lines shows her to mean also calculated eloquence, artful speech, a distinction revealing that she has entered the fallen world because she has conceived for the first time of the willful manipulation of language."[32] Thus though she decides to share the fruit with Adam only after she has second thoughts about the force of the proscription, she assumes the guise of selflessness as Satan has of love: "for thee / Chiefly I sought" (IX.877-878), she tells Adam. Further, having sinned in the hope of reversing their positions, she now invites him to accept from her the gift of equality. He must "also taste," she insists, "that equal Lot / May join us, equal Joy, as equal Love" (IX.881-882), repeating the adjective that should evoke from Adam not acquiescence but abhorrence.

Yet despite the precocity with which she learns Satan's art, Adam is overcome not by her arguments but by his attraction to her person: "The Bond of Nature draw me to my own, / My own in thee, for what thou art is mine; / Our State cannot be sever'd, we are one, / One Flesh; to lose thee were to lose myself" (IX.956-959). In a sense, though, Eve's appeal is parallel to her argument. The misleading verbal facade she presents is analogous to the physical form of a marriage that lacks spiritual harmony, a union which is, as Milton had argued repeatedly, no marriage at all. As Eve ignores Raphael's lesson on Satan's ability to manipulate language, so Adam chooses to forget the corollaries, that external appearance may disguise internal reality and that patience and obedience are the appropriate responses to apparent impasse.

In *Paradise Lost* we do not see Adam as we do Eve practicing the suasive rhetoric their fall has made available to humanity, but the effect of Original Sin on his speech is nonetheless clear. Although wordplay is common in Edenic speech, it works before the Fall to emphasize the concord of words and their referents. In fallen speech, however, punning shows the distance that Satan's calculation has introduced between *res* and *verba*. Eve begins to pun in demonic fashion immediately upon seeing the tree. Where the narrator's use of the word "Fruit" from the first lines of the poem has been to stress how its double meaning is complementary, Eve's verbal play introduces a tension between the two senses: "Serpent, we might have spar'd our coming hither, / Fruitless to mee, though Fruit be here to excess" (IX.647-648). After the Fall, Adam complicates this effect, obscuring real difference with verbal similarity as Satan and Belial do. He immediately puns on "sapience," and though he has lost the insight that had allowed him to name the creatures accurately, Adam invents etymologies to degrade Eve's character: "woman" means now "Man's woe" (XI.632), "Eve" associated with "evil" (IX.1067).[33] And if before the Fall "conversation" suggests all the kinds of proper, loving intercourse between man and woman, so after their sin love becomes fornication, verbal exchange only "mutual accusation" (IX.1187). As a measure of his intellectual degeneration, Adam begins his most vitriolic tirade against Eve with the abusive and inappropriate epithet "thou Serpent" (X.867). Thus the language Satan has invented in the war in heaven becomes current among human beings as well, words no longer existing in order to express and celebrate truth but only to attack and misrepresent.

CHAPTER THREE

Michael, Adam, and the Means of Revelation

I N *Paradise Lost* the distance between God and fallen humanity is presented as a linguistic gap. Through their sin Adam and Eve forfeit the inner image of their maker, the imprint of the divine Word which their Edenic language has expressed. Consequently their conversation becomes abusive and inaccurate, their prayers inarticulate. Royal Society philosophers argued that what had been lost through a lapse in reason, reason can restore, but for Milton the Fall was too radically damaging for humans to recover from its effects without heavenly assistance. The human couple requires the Son to translate their prayers, rendering their sighs intelligible, but even this feeble attempt to approach God depends upon a dispensation of "Prevenient Grace" (XI.3). The function of this newly "implanted Grace" (XI.23), however, is not to restore the spontaneous clarity and eloquence of prelapsarian speech. Milton's Adam and Eve have never lived in the paradise of denotative language seventeenth-century linguists hoped to regain, but even the various, poetic style which they have practiced is inadequate to the complexities and ambiguities of the world their sin has brought about. Thus if the rectitude of human words, the power of language to communicate God and serve him, is to be recovered, it must be on terms fundamentally different from those obtaining in Eden.

As opposed to the complex style which dominates most of the epic, Milton concludes his poem with a relatively straightforward summary, first through vision and then through Michael's narrative, of the history of Adam's heirs from the Fall to the coming of Christ and beyond. The shift is surprising and has proved distasteful to many readers, some of whom see here a rejection of epic splendor in favor of the "plain style" endorsed by Puritan preachers and Restoration linguists. But just as we must view the war in heaven both from Adam's perspective and from our own, so in the last books if we adopt a dual stance we can recognize, first, that Michael's style and method are dictated by the needs and limitations of his primary audience; and second, that the last books actually serve to justify the more elaborate style of the rest of the poem, revealing it as an appropriate means to convey divine truths to fallen readers.

In prelapsarian Eden, Creation itself had intimated the signs of divinity which helped to sustain Adam's innocence, but the Fall has both marred the text of "the Book of knowledge fair" (III.47) and obscured Adam's perceptive faculties. As a consequence of Adam's sin, the vehicle for human regeneration must differ from, or at least supplement, whatever indications of God's beneficence remain in the natural order. Milton's readers share their first father's diminished capacity, but because they already know what Adam is encountering for the first time, the epic narrator can use words commemoratively, evoking the full range of the readers' knowledge as he extends and enriches their understanding of God's ways. Michael, however, must bring his pupil to the same vantage point through a slow and painful process, using the indicative force of words to disabuse Adam of the preconceptions he still carries with him while at the same time instilling in him the means for detecting God's design in the new world his sin has brought about.

Like the poet contemplating his epic strategy, Michael and Adam must survey the means at their disposal in search of a medium adequate both to convey the knowledge necessary for salvation and to address effectively the fallen human capacity for knowing. Adam grows in maturity and wisdom as Michael leads him to appreciate the insufficiency of beauty and power as

indices to spiritual worth, and he turns therefore from revelation
in Nature to revelation in history. What the creating Word had
provided in the Garden, he learns, Christ the Redeemer will
supply in historical time. But if the promise of Incarnation and
Apocalypse lends chronological time an optimistic design, still
for each individual the anticipated redemption of the race is not
entirely adequate. Rather, history must be internalized, its
shape and significant events turned to biography in which Christ
is immanent as well as anticipated. It is not, then, history *per se*
but its message for each soul that is important, and this message
is available only in Scripture and expounded only from the
pulpits of God's consecrated ministers. Thus the Word emerges
as the only medium appropriate to save humanity, to establish
the paradise within, and this conclusion to Michael's survey not
only dictates the strictly narrative presentation of Book XII, but
together with the rest of the vision it also legitimizes Milton's
enterprise and the method he employs to achieve his epic
purpose.

[I]

Even before Michael's arrival, Adam has glimpsed the fact
that history provides the source of renewed hope, and at the
same time he begins to understand that language, if it is to be a
medium for God's revelation in the fallen world, must assume a
more complex function than Edenic speech. Stimulated by Eve's
desire to avert or limit the penalty, Adam recalls the curse on the
serpent, "Her Seed shall bruise thy head, thou bruise his heel"
(X.181), and he recognizes that it contains as well a prophecy of
redemption.[1] This new interpretation of the Son's words is the
work of the Interior Teacher, who by restoring his hope moves
Adam to pray for forgiveness. A subsequent result is the partial
recovery of Adam's verbal facility, for although the Word must
translate the inarticulate sighs of the human couple to God the
Father, when their prayer is finished, Adam feels confirmed in
his reading of the curse and promptly addresses Eve once more
by her original title. While after the Fall he has begun his

vitriolic tirade against her with the inappropriate epithet "thou Serpent" (X.867), once he realizes that she is to be the instrument for Satan's undoing, he restores her rightful name, exclaiming, "Hail to thee, / *Eve* rightly call'd, Mother of all Mankind, / Mother of all things living, since by thee / Man is to live, and all things live for Man" (XI.158-161). Anne Ferry has said of the recovered speech of Adam and Eve, "The instrument of redemption is language purified of Satanic abuses and restored to its creative eloquence."[2] But Adam can no longer speak an Edenic language. The words may be the same in form, but their significance has been enlarged by the altered circumstances in which Adam finds himself.

In Paradise words have no real etymology, just as Adam has no real history, and consequently Adam's verbal precision is unself-conscious, unaware of the dualism which makes the congruence of sign and thing all the more striking to Milton's readers. But after the Fall, words like people acquire a temporal dimension, which is a primary source of their potential ambiguity. Thus though Adam replaces "Serpent" with "Eve" he cannot forget the complex associations with the serpent that his wife now evokes, an association made unavoidable for Adam by the fact that in Hebrew the two words are homonyms.[3] If he infers "Serpent" from "Eve," however, he must remember both the Fall and the promised victory. And so redeemed language exploits the ambiguities the Fall interjects into human existence, turning tragic implications to hopeful ones. The recovery of Adam's speech is the product of an illumination supplied by the inner Word, but the fuller implications of Adam's insight must be elaborated, the means of the prophecy's fulfillment explored before Adam is capable of profiting from the complexities of redeemed speech as the epic narrator uses it. He must first perceive God's working in time, learning through a dialectic between the inner Word and its historical manifestations rather than its revelation in Nature. And for that process to be effective, Michael as mediator must become relatively transparent, his style accommodated to the flaws of perception it is his mission to rectify.

Michael's speech may be straightforward, but his method of instruction is in its own way as oblique as the narrator's, using

Adam's response to negative visions as a means of leading him to positive alternatives. Before he can comprehend the necessity for a new mode of revelation, Adam must first experience the failure of his previous assumptions to deal with the circumstances prevailing in the fallen world. Pleasure is the affective result of beauty, and the innocent delights of the divine Creation suggest that Milton's Eden approximates very closely the condition Samuel Johnson would reserve only for a higher realm: "The happiness of Heaven will be, that pleasure and virtue will be perfectly consistent."[4] But the distinction that remains between the Eden Milton describes and the Heaven Johnson anticipates must be respected. Raphael has warned in Book VIII that the enjoyment of lesser goods, however pleasurable and proper in their own right, contains a potential for abuse; one must look not to the gift but to the giver. And even then, the created object is never an adequate reflection of the Creator. The agility of his unfallen mind notwithstanding, Adam requires expositors in Eden to supplement with definitive information the sense of divinity Nature intimates to him and to keep him from accepting any of Creation's beauties as final.[5] After the Fall, his incapacity to penetrate to the meaning underlying the images Michael presents is both more acute and more dangerous. As their sexual abandon after their first sin demonstrates, the fallen Adam and Eve have a greater propensity to subvert reason to appetite, and so they must approach the sources of pleasure with a caution they had never before been required to exercise.

In Adam's prelapsarian existence, pleasure and virtue are at least a part of the same continuum if not identical, and it is with the memory of that innocent condition still defining his address to the world that he turns from the ugliness of death and disease to take solace in the beauty of the "spacious Plain" (XI.556). But the attractive surface, Michael warns him, is only a facade concealing moral degeneration:

> Judge not what is best
> By pleasure, though to Nature seeming meet,
> Created, as thou art, to nobler end
> Holy and pure, conformity divine.

Those Tents thou saw'st so pleasant, were the Tents
Of wickedness, wherein shall dwell his Race
Who slew his Brother; studious they appear
Of Arts that polish Life, Inventors rare,
Unmindful of thir Maker, though his Spirit
Taught them, but they his gifts acknowledg'd none.
Yet they a beauteous offspring shall beget;
For that fair female Troop thou saw'st, that seem'd
Of Goddesses, so blithe, so smooth, so gay
Yet empty of all good wherein consists
Woman's domestic honor and chief praise;
Bred only and completed to the taste
Of lustful appetence, to sing, to dance,
To dress, and troll the Tongue, and roll the Eye.
To these that sober Race of Men, whose lives
Religious titl'd them the Sons of God,
Shall yield up all thir virtue, all thir fame
Ignobly, to the trains and to the smiles
Of these fair Atheists, and now swim in joy,
(Erelong to swim at large) and laugh; for which
The world erelong a world of tears must weep.

(XI. 603-627)

   As he does repeatedly in Book XI, Adam here mistakes
appearance for reality, libertinism for lawful pleasure. Because
appetite gains control so easily over fallen reason, Adam must
learn restraint through discipline where once he had practiced
temperance spontaneously. The course of Michael's exposition
acquaints Adam with the distinction the fallen world enforces
between physical representation and spiritual truth. And aesthetic appeal, as a potential effect of physical representation, must
be regarded as a more dubious index to worth than it had been
in Eden, where until Satan's invasion beauty had signified
divinity even if it did not subsume it. Adam's response to the first
vision Michael shows him is aesthetic in the fullest sense; he
recoils from Cain's murder of Abel not only because of an
aversion to physical pain but also because he is repulsed by its
ugliness:[6]

But have I now seen Death? Is this the way
I must return to native dust? O sight
Of terror, foul and ugly to behold,
Horrid to think, how horrible to feel!   (XI.462-465)

Michael's reply corrects this response, divorcing the fact of death from its "many shapes" (XI.467) and its sensory threshold from its quiescent inner sanctum: "yet to sense / More terrible at th'entrance than within" (XI.469-470). Adam's repulsion at the "unsightly sufferings" (XI.510) the Lazar house discloses is also aesthetic, but in the elaborative dialogue that ensues, he evinces some development. Striving to reconcile the human deformity he sees with the notion of the creation of human beings *ad imaginem Dei*, he shows a desire to transcend a troubling event in order to arrive at the truth which it reflects only obscurely and with considerable distortion. Michael's answer to Adam's question, though hardly definitive, is nonetheless appropriate to the iconoclastic temper of the book because it denies any necessary and immutable investiture of temporal reality with spiritual significance (XI.515-525). This same point Michael reiterates when, in describing the displacement during the flood of the mountain on which Paradise was situated, he explains, "God áttributes to place / No sanctity, if none be thither brought / By Men who there frequent, or therein dwell" (XI.836-838). Viewing the "spacious Plain" Adam again commits the aesthetic fallacy, attributing to feminine beauty a power to convey meaning that the ugliness of death has been shown to lack. Disabused of that notion, he embraces a more abstract but finally self-serving revaluation, blaming man's woes on woman, which Michael's curt reply corrects: "From Man's effeminate slackness it begins, / Said th'Angel, who should better hold his place / By wisdom, and superior gifts receiv'd" (XI.634-636).

Adam's excessive devotion to Eve has warned us against the reliability of the aesthetic responses on which he recurrently depends in Book XI, and the attractiveness of the lost Eden makes us understand the force of the longing that causes him to require Michael's repeated corrections. If the use of pleasure as a norm to guide action results in the hedonism of the debauched priests, which is a local manifestation of Sin, so there is an equally specious alternative whose prototype is Death. Like aesthetic appeal, physical power has even before the Fall been revealed as an inadequate index to the legitimacy of the positions it enforces. Abdiel's puzzlement that Satan, bereft of angelic goodness, should still enjoy angelic "strength and might" (VI.116) foreshadows the repellent treatment of Cain's sin and its civilized counterpart, war. Adam's horror is of course aesthetic, at least initially, but the epic voice provides direction for the incipient militarists in Milton's audience, dismissing summarily the displays of military prowess with "On each hand slaughter and gigantic deeds" (XI.659). Juxtaposed to these spectacles, and overshadowing them morally if not physically, is the recurrent figure of the "one just man," a type of the isolated and humble Christ of *Paradise Regained*.[7]

Michael teaches not merely through negative images or positive, if humble examples, but by explicitly supplementing these images with their doctrinal import in order to correct Adam's untutored response to them. This procedure has much in common with Puritan sermonizing, but the balance of particular with general is characteristic of another didactic literary mode equally important to Puritans: spiritual history and its subgenre, spiritual biography.[8] The Puritan interest in the past has its doctrinal basis in the Calvinist resistance to natural theology. Revelation in Creation is still objectively real, but to fallen people it can be only a reminder of their guilt and not a way to regeneration. The revelation in history, recorded in the Scriptures, is what matters, and only through it can people hope to decipher the Book of Nature accurately. But like the revelation in Creation, historical revelation also requires careful exposition in order to convey the proper lessons. As image is to visual perception, so event is to historical study; neither is self-sufficient, both must be explicated. The Puritan interest in history, then, lay not in the raw data of temporal experience but in its capacity for instruction. The bias against the potential for idolatry latent in icon making did not extend to the transmission of history, partly because the latter is most effectively mediated verbally. Still, their use of history, exploiting its homiletic potential, suggests its affinity with the treatment of the image in Puritan hermeneutics, which Milo Kaufmann has studied with respect to *The Pilgrim's Progress*:

> Since there was no truth in the image *per se*, it had to be discounted; the truth lay in an abstraction from the image, an abstraction that might be equated to word, and that abstraction in turn had as its referent the *true* object, which was an abstraction from the object as it existed in protean variousness for the imagination. Revelation, bypassing images entirely, might use words which related referents without taint of distortion or ambiguity.[9]

This process of abstraction leads to an emphasis on concept or precept, using only sufficient detail to give the lesson force for the listener. Fullness of account is sacrificed in order to gain the perspective from which those details most illustrative of the doctrinal truth of the event stand in sharpest outline. The geographical counterpart to this intellectual attitude is, of course, Michael's mountain, where the distance renders the typological truth of history more apparent because, like images, types are explicable only in terms of a conceptual analogy with their antitype.[10] A pedagogical method which eschews detail in favor of precepts depends heavily upon memory, the ability to recall lessons revealed in history, as well as upon reason, the ability to choose the appropriate lesson and apply it correctly in one's life. The details of spiritual biography serve as an aid to empathetic appreciation of the trials of our ancestors, a quality Adam reveals in his compassion for the suffering of his progeny in the Lazar house and at the Flood. But the point, Michael's continued tutelage seems to indicate, lies elsewhere, in the general which gives meaning to the particular. Recalling the lives of God's people in all ages helps the person of faith to recognize the signs of his or her own redemption, and reflection on the promise of the Second Coming, the assurance that history has both a meaning and a goal, is a way of transcending the tribulations of the moment. Thus Michael's pedagogy, whether its substance is vision or narrative, relies upon the same method for its effect. Because it is through verbal exposition that meaning is implanted in the mind and kept alive there most effectively, Michael repeatedly deflects Adam's attention, as Milton often does ours, from its potential engrossment in the event to the transcendent meaning which neither event nor image can successfully embody.

Yet Michael's purpose is not to teach Adam how to interpret history but how to turn from spectator to participant without surrendering his sense of the paradise within. Consequently Michael does not simply offer precepts for Adam to memorize so much as he involves his pupil in the often laborious process of discovering for himself the truths which underlie the presentation. The lesson that Raphael has taught through astronomy, Michael uses history to impart. Thus however closely Michael imitates Puritan models, he also qualifies as an expert practitioner of the Socratic method, acquainting his pupil with the limits of his knowledge while engaging him in a quest for its perfection.[11] As Adam has made an effort to extract meaning from the exposure of the allurements of the "spacious Plain," so when he sees the rainbow at the conclusion of the deluge, he again ventures an interpretation, this time more adequate if not entirely sufficient. But his attitude is as important as his answer. Where before he had been assertive and self-serving, here his hypotheses are offered in an interrogative mode, signaling his willingness to submit to an authority more trustworthy than his own reason.[12] Instead of reproving, then, Michael praises him and confirms the substance of his insight while elaborating its further implications:

> Dext'rously thou aim'st;
> So willingly doth God remit his Ire,
> Though late repenting him of Man deprav'd,
> Griev'd at his heart, when looking down he saw
> The whole Earth fill'd with violence, and all flesh
> Corrupting each thir way; yet those remov'd,
> Such grace shall one just Man find in his sight,
> That he relents, not to blot out mankind,
> And makes a Cov'nant never to destroy
> The Earth again by flood, nor let the Sea

Surpass his bounds, nor Rain to drown the World
With Man therein or Beast; but when he brings
Over the Earth a Cloud, will therein set
His triple-color'd Bow, whereon to look
And call to mind his Cov'nant.   (XI.884-898)

Like the events Adam has been watching, even divinely
sanctioned images cannot embody spiritual truths, but properly
explicated they can lead the observer to discover those truths in
himself.

[II]

Much of Book XI is devoted to exposing the aesthetic fallacy, the
presumption that Beauty is Truth, to which Adam has shown
himself to be especially subject both before and after the Fall. As
a corollary, the vision also dismisses the military fallacy, the
assertion that might makes right. Adam's response to the latter
continues to be at least partly aesthetic: it is the spectacle of war
that disgusts him. But Milton's readers, acquainted with the
qualities most prized in classical epic and having witnessed
conflicts close in time, are expected to supplement Adam's
primarily intuitive response with moral revulsion. The content of
the vision then works as a kind of negative formula. In consonance with the psychological theory that like banishes like, to
which Milton subscribes in the preface to *Samson Agonistes*,
Michael objectifies alternatives to the way of life he is espousing
as a means of purging Adam of the desire to pursue them. The
same principle is put to a more compressed use in Milton's epic
similes, which often proceed negatively, as when in the initial
description of Eden Milton carefully excludes the most famous
false paradises:

Not that fair field
Of *Enna*, where *Proserpin* gath'ring flow'rs
Herself a fairer Flow'r by gloomy *Dis*
Was gather'd, which cost *Ceres* all that pain

To seek her through the world; nor that sweet Grove
Of *Daphne* by *Orontes*, and th' inspir'd
Castalian Spring might with this Paradise
Of *Eden* strive; nor that *Nyseian* Isle
Girt with the River *Triton*, where old *Cham*,
Whom Gentiles *Ammon* call and *Lybian Jove*,
Hid *Amalthea* and her Florid Son,
Young *Bacchus*, from his Stepdame *Rhea's* eye;
Nor where *Abassin* Kings thir issue Guard,
Mount *Amara*, though this by some suppos'd
True Paradise under the *Ethiop* Line
By *Nilus* head, enclos'd with shining Rock,
A whole day's journey high, but wide remote
From this *Assyrian* Garden . . .   (IV. 268-285)

But the more extended use of the technique, common in the last
books, is characteristic also of *Paradise Regained* and *Samson
Agonistes*. As Adam's vision varies the prospects of sensual indulgence and glory in battle, so both Samson and Christ are
tempted with physical ease and temporal success. Christ, of
course, has no real need for this moral catharsis; he submits to it
for the sake of Milton's readers, so that through him we are
cleansed. For fallen humanity, however, the objectification of
evil is necessary for the working of grace. Like Moses' laws as
Michael describes their function, the inadequacy of what is
presented externally convinces the observer of the need to rely
solely on the Redeemer as the way to recover the paradise
within:

And therefore was Law given them to evince
Thir natural pravity, by stirring up
Sin against Law to fight; that when they see
Law can discover sin, but not remove,
Save by those shadowy expiations weak,
The blood of Bulls and Goats, they may conclude
Some blood more precious must be paid for Man,
Just for unjust, that in such righteousness
To them by Faith imputed, they may find

Justification towards God, and peace
Of Conscience, which the Law by Ceremonies
Cannot appease, nor Man the moral part
Perform, and not performing cannot live.   (XII.287-299)

In Book XI Adam grows from a dependence upon disconnected pageant to an appreciation of the essential continuity of
history as it moves to fulfill God's redemptive purpose. But the
historical sense has its dangers as well. In the vision, civilization
is treated with suspicion. Augustine notes that human cities
inevitably bear the brand of Cain: "It is recorded of Cain that he
built a city, but Abel, being a sojourner, built none."[13] The
substance of civilization is the subordination of nature to art in
conjunction with, and usually only as a result of, military prowess; and the outrage of Enoch and Noah shows that worldly
beauty and power are simply metonyms for Sin and Death. The
Flood is inadequate to erase the mark of Cain from the human
city, but after the waters subside, God's intervention seems
about to establish the good society, to provide a civilization
capable of conveying His truth and establishing it in history.
The seed of Abraham, the people Moses and Joshua lead to
Canaan, the constituents of David all seem at first to offer a
viable alternative to the potential vehicles for truth which have
already been dismissed. But the hope turns out to be ephemeral,
the people themselves too morally wayward, to meet literally the
expectations they evoke. Rather, the chiliastic fallacy must also
be purged, the law of Moses must be superseded and the earthly
kingdom transformed by the antitype of these leaders into a
kingdom of the spirit and not of the world.

The view of history, then, is eschatological without being
progressive in the evolutionary sense. Causation, the mechanical
sequentiality of events, is granted to Satan, as Michael will later
comment: "so shall the World go on, / To good malignant, to
bad men benign" (XII. 537-538). But the *ordo naturae* is still
ultimately God's, and it is as capable of encompassing His
miraculous incursions in the fallen, historical world as it is of
determining the results of the Fall.[14] The process of causation
and incursion in history is like the presentation in Book XI in

terms of episode and explication. It is neither history's meaning-less flux nor its simple repetitions that are finally important, but rather the miracle of illumination which transcends history.

Michael's summary treatment of postdiluvian time, in which the Word exists as a promise but is not yet incarnate, empha-sizes transcendent meaning. The tenuous hold of the seed of Abraham on worldly glory precludes the establishment of the Israelite nation as a permanent vehicle for God's truth, but it does suggest the nature of the medium which will supplant it. Moses' fortitude looks beyond itself to Christ in a number of ways: in the law, which Adam himself recognizes is inadequate; in the wandering in the wilderness, a type of the experience which Milton will make the subject of his brief epic; and in the succession, at the entrance to Canaan, of "*Joshua* whom the Gentiles *Jesus* call" (XII.310). Similarly, David's stock will produce the later Jesus to rule over a different kind of kingdom. Thus history yields its figurative meaning just as the Creation did to Adam's eager inquiries, but Michael's presentation shows that though the tenor lends the vehicle its significance, the meaning is inseparable from the process of its discovery.

Accompanying the internalization in the last books is a stylistic shift from the practice of the earlier account which has met with widespread disapprobation. C.S. Lewis, for instance, has called the whole of Michael's presentation "an untransmuted lump of futur-ity" in which "the structural effect . . . is inartistic" and "the actual writing . . . curiously bad." Lewis speculated that a number of extrinsic factors might account for what he regarded as a failure in poetic power:

> Perhaps Milton was in ill health. Perhaps, being old, he yielded to a natural, though disastrous, impatience to get the work finished. And since he was writing in a very new manner, he probably had no useful criticism—no one to tell him that the style of these last books bore only a superficial resemblance to that of his epic prime. [15]

But the relative lack of ceremonial grandeur surrounding Mi-chael's appearance suggests that the shift represents Milton's

deliberate choice to adopt the style Lewis so deplores. In contrast to the elaborate and reciprocal greetings which Raphael's
visit elicits, here Michael responds only perfunctorily to Adam's
gesture: "*Adam* bow'd low, hee Kingly from his State / Inclin'd
not, but his coming thus declar'd. / *Adam*, Heav'n's high behest
no Preface needs" (XI.249-251). Michael's succinctness signals
both a change in man's relation to the divine and the new
strictures that the shift places upon language, exigencies which
are reflected in the muted style.

In part, the alteration is traceable to the models of historical
and biographical accounts which are apparent in these books,
for the essence of their style is a lack of overt adornment. An
important convention of Puritan hagiographical writings, William Haller has pointed out, "was that they should seem to
possess no art but the art of the holy spirit, which was simply to
report the facts." The medium does not call attention to itself
because it seeks, like the "mathematical style" of the Royal
Society, to be perfectly transparent, absorbed as fully as possible
into the content. For this reason, Haller explains, such Puritans
as Baxter could commend history "much as humanist critics
like Sidney had praised poetry, for being both 'useful' and
'delightful.' "[16] In part, too, the style is a function of the historical time which the Fall has brought about. In the Garden,
time had existed only as a medium of infinite growth, and its
"grateful vicissitude" is reflected in the elaborate and ceremonious language Milton uses to describe it. Here, time is to
be transcended, and Michael's succinctness, because it pays
such single-minded attention to its purpose, precludes our absorption in the moment at hand.

Most important, though, is Adam's lack of intellectual subtlety, which makes his case a special one and Michael's style
therefore inappropriate as a model for more general application.
Accustomed to the purely referential language he had employed
in Eden, Adam is not yet equipped to turn to effective use the
ambiguities of diction and syntax Milton trusts his readers to
appreciate through most of the epic. Adam must come, guided
by Michael, to approximate the reader's sophistication. Unlike
his Christian heirs, Adam is capable of typological interpretation

only in retrospect: the manifestation of the antitype alone can invest the type with symbolic meaning, and he acquires this knowledge gradually, constantly revaluating what is retained in his memory in the light of new information. But the reader is under no such constraint. Prodded by Michael's insinuations, which must for a time remain cryptic to Adam, we can see through the historical event to the truth for which it is a shadowy type. Thus the alternation of glorious evil with humble virtue functions as a latent epic simile much as the opposing views of astronomy function for Adam in Book VIII, as stages in a process of supersession leading to what is beyond all comparison. And a part of the intended satisfaction for the reader must lie in our compassionate understanding of his perplexity mixed with the confidence that he will progress as readily as we and with the relief that we are long past the initiation he is undergoing.

If Milton modulates his epic voice from a sense of decorum, he is likewise in these last books offering a justification of his earlier style. As Ben Jonson had argued in his famous quarrel with Inigo Jones, unless the primacy of the word is carefully protected, it will fall victim to spectacle, the experience of which is inevitably ephemeral and potentially misleading.[17] Adam's recurrent absorption in the pageants of Book XI constitutes a proof of Jonson's point and also explains why the shows of Hell and the genuine glory of Eden alike are always subject to the controlling and correcting voice of the bard. The greater energy and elaboration of the earlier books has been required in order to accommodate an alien experience to his fallen readers. Given an Adam new to history, Michael presents time spatially; given a readership whose sensibilities have been shaped by the flux of linear time, Milton through simile and allusion temporalizes Edenic space. But despite the complementary techniques, the effect is the same. For Adam as for his heirs, the mode of presentation is a stimulus both to affirm the revelation in history and to stand apart from the local and immediate incidents of its unfolding.

In Book XI, image has been subordinated to concept in response to the limitations of human epistemology. In Book XII, however, spectacle subsides altogether, to be replaced with narrative. Louis Martz is among the critics who deplore Michael's pedagogical strategy:

> . . . if the reader is expected to grasp the workings of grace
> against sin, they must somehow be given an adequate ima-
> gistic and dramatic presentation, to counter the powerful
> thrust of the scenes of sin. Milton has done exactly this in
> Book 10, in presenting the recovery of Adam and Eve. Here
> he fails to present any such organic vision, and instead
> allows a fissure to develop between the concrete represen-
> tations of sin and the abstract assertions of Adam's
> "Teacher."[18]

The concession to local effect that Martz desires, however, would destroy the larger, conceptual unity of the poem, which is dependent not upon image and drama but upon the elucidating word. Throughout the poem, Milton has reserved the most sharply delineated images to the presentation of Hell, to Satan and his constituents, and the most compelling drama to the results of their plotting. Even in Eden and Heaven, where outer form and inner reality exist in concord, the explicating word is ultimately controlling, while in the last books the distance between image and truth amounts to a hellish abyss. Because in a fallen world, and to fallen eyes, images constitute a particularly dangerous attempt to render the spiritual, Milton must resort once more to the negative formula which has served him thus far. Like the earlier images of beauty and power, the worldly kingdom of David is ephemeral, but though we reject the chiliastic fallacy along with the aesthetic and the military, we come to accept the spiritual kingdom it typifies.

Corresponding to the altered method of Book XII is an explicit concern with the verbal medium, for Michael's narration begins with Nimrod's Babel and concludes with Pentecost. Commentators define the tower in various ways. Boehme, for instance, allegorizes it as a symbol of human pride: "This *Towre* . . . is a *figure* of the fallen earthly man who is entered into Selfehood." For Luther, however, Nimrod is the founder of "the false and deceitful church which proved itself the source of all (*other*) ungodliness."[19] Whatever its specific meaning, Protestants are generally agreed that it represents an attempt to supplant the Word of God with a human artifact. Fallen man, Boehme declares, "hath made the formed word of God *in* him, unto an *Idoll*; for the nature of the *Towre* was even this; *viz.* that it should there stand as a great *wonder*, which men had made in their own contriving *Phancy*, whereupon they would *ascend up to God;* and signifies, that man hath *lost* the right understanding of God and his habitation and essence."[20] Thus God's curse sealed in speech the confusion that had already occurred in thought, making the letter conform to the spirit.

But if Babel is the verbal equivalent to the Fall, Pentecost is the dispensation which counters the curse, converting the degeneration of language to a *felix culpa.* Although "The diversity of tongues did hinder the gospel from being spread abroad any farther," according to Calvin,

> God invented a way whereby it might break out, when he divided and clove the tongues of the apostles, that they might spread that abroad amongst all people which was delivered to them. Wherein appeareth the manifold goodness of God, because a plague and punishment of man's pride was turned into matter of blessing.[21]

And Luther, arguing against Reformation provincialism, points out, "The Holy Spirit . . . did not wait till all the world came to Jerusalem and studied Hebrew, but gave manifold tongues for the office of the ministry, so that the apostles could preach wherever they might go."[22] Milton is even more positive, arguing in his *Art of Logic* that all languages, "both that first one which Adam spoke in Eden, and those varied ones . . . which the builders of the tower of Babel suddenly received, are without doubt divinely given" (CE, 11: 221). The study of other languages, consequently, is a divine imperative, and by the same token one's own tongue must also be cultivated, its resources extended so that it may convey what is otherwise incommunicable.

As Michael and Adam struggle through a series of commonly offered though failed alternatives to the Word as a way to mediate saving knowledge to fallen human beings, we are made to see also the choices confronting the epic poet. In the last books of *Paradise Lost*, Milton stands apart from the elements characteristic of his epic style, and in so doing he exposes to us the perspective from which he transcends, purifies, and reclaims the poetic traditions he draws upon. Lacking the experience of Babel and Pentecost, Adam is not capable of appreciating the insight Milton's etymological puns offer to his readers; and unsophisticated as he is at the beginning of the vision, he must be purged of his attraction to beauty, power, and religious utopia, enticements whose lure even the soberest and most mature minds must occasionally feel. Nonetheless, the fallen mind we share with Adam dictates both the plain style of Michael's sermon and the dense, often oblique poetry we are accustomed to hearing from Milton's bardic voice. Coming to the fallen world with Edenic preconceptions still informing his vision, Adam requires Michael's clarity. Milton's readers, however, though they are no less fallen than Adam, are more accustomed to the world he is seeing for the first time, and they are therefore appropriately addressed through a language whose complexity approximates the nature of their experience. Yet neither in substance nor in method are the angelic and the bardic narrators as far apart as they seem. Despite the dangers they present, Milton can make use of images and historical allusions because like Michael he consistently refuses to let us accept them as sufficient analogies for his "higher Argument" (IX.42) but only as first terms in a progression, external, negative formulations which lead us to an ever-increasing knowledge of the indwelling Word.

CHAPTER FOUR

Recovering the Word

❦

The Ethics of Intention and the Warrant for Action in Comus *and* Paradise Regained

In *Paradise Lost* Milton charts Adam's verbal development, tracing his descent from the clarity and suggestiveness of Edenic speech to the distortions and misrepresentations fallen language admits. If Raphael in narrating the war in heaven anticipates the ways in which human language will be corrupted, however, Michael in the last books demonstrates that redeemed speech, words sanctified by the Word, becomes the most suitable vehicle for truth in the fallen world. But despite the unique opportunity the epic presents for the exploration of this topic, Milton's interest in corrupt speech and the terms upon which it may be restored to divine use is revealed throughout his career and most particularly in all the temptation poems. The protagonists in the other three poems, as well as the narrator in *Paradise Lost*, are all the heirs of Adam's sin, and they each confront a world defined by Satan or by his representatives. Yet just as the fallen Adam is led to the truth by discovering the inadequacy of what is false, so the other protagonists by contending with the words of erring speakers come to recover the divine Word.

As Milton's combative prose bears witness, speech is to him a form of action, and in order to express divine purpose it must be predicated upon the same spiritual circumstances that make all acts worthy. Adam's prayers must be translated by the Word in order to be intelligible in heaven, and similarly in *Comus* the beauty of the Lady's singing, as well as the power of her speech, reflects the divine source of her inspiration. But though in Protestantism it is the spiritual state, the intention, rather than the act itself that determines its moral value, still the mere confirmation of the Lady's virtue is a goal insufficient either to the necessities of reformation or to the occasion of the masque. Consequently, once she has demonstrated the complete self-denial on which the life of faith is predicated, she must be freed from her paralysis in order to serve God through charitable action. If the Lady's trial and release define the stages of the spiritual progress leading ultimately to good works, it remains, however, for Christ in *Paradise Regained* to demonstrate how the heavenly warrant for action is exercised within a vocation whose primary tool is language. As he resists Satan's temptations, he discovers at the same time the terms on which his ministry is to be conducted, the means to convey the miracle he has been called to express.

[I]

Like the confusing panorama Adam faces in the final books of *Paradise Lost*, Comus's Wood is a version of the world Original Sin brings into existence. The symbolism in the masque is certainly elusive, the facets of its meaning incapable of being exhausted within the limits of a single system of thought. But if most commentators find in Christian doctrine an appropriate vocabulary for describing the central conflict and its resolution, still the kind of Christianity generally employed is less than adequate to the world the masque evokes. Most Christian interpretations have imputed to the masque the natural theology of Anglicanism and have thus credited Nature with supplying the ethical standard on the basis of which the Lady resists Comus's temptations. Grace enters only to reward her perseverance, not to initiate or sustain it.[1] Milton's presentation, however, adheres more closely to the strict Calvinist view, which holds that the Book of Nature has been obscured by the Fall, its text susceptible to ambiguity or to the misconstructions Satanic figures can impose; and as a result of the inadequacies of fallen vision, we cannot even begin to be Virtue's "true Servants" (10) without first receiving grace as a gift from God.

The inconclusiveness of natural signs is evident from the first. Long before Comus arrives to argue for a definition of Nature she cannot accept, the Lady discovers that the interpretation of phenomena is a function more of the perceiving mind than of the thing perceived. As her fears grow and her brothers fail to return, she attributes to nightfall increasingly sinister motives. Counterpointing Comus's celebration of darkness as "Il Penseroso" counterpoints "L'Allegro," she converts the "sad Votarist in Palmer's weed" into first "envious darkness" and finally "thievish Night" (189-195). She regains her composure when she recognizes that her fears are due to creatures of her own devising, thoughts that "may startle well, but not astound / The virtuous mind" (210-211). The appearance of Chastity verifies her resolution, but though it has a force and reality the phantasms do not, the "unblemish't form" (215) is nonetheless a reflection of her own mind, a projection which reveals more about her character than about the world in which she finds herself.

Just as the Lady's inability to derive a clear meaning from the world around her suggests a Calvinist reluctance to accept natural theology, so the power which sustains her virtue indicates a strict adherence to the Protestant doctrine of justification by faith. For Luther and his followers all virtue is predicated upon faith, which is in turn the result of a free dispensation of grace. Accordingly Milton grounds the Lady's perseverance not in a doctrine extracted from Nature but in the grace with which she enters the Wood. Lacking its illuminating effect, Comus cannot give a precise name to the Lady's special quality, but even he can recognize from her song that "something holy lodges in that breast" (246), and he later testifies to the chilling force of that same "superior power" (801) as she refutes his argument. Like Luther, then, Milton presents grace as not simply the culmination of a Christian life but its sustenance as well. In Protestant theology, however, there are kinds of grace corresponding to the stages in the ascent to complete regeneration.

The grace that leads Adam and Eve to pray is only the enabling "prevenient grace" that allows one to begin the process of sanctification. But the power that Comus detects in the Lady's song and speech is the subsequent grace that permits one to persevere in faith. William Perkins distinguishes between "preventing" and "cooperating" grace as agents of the two types of conversion:

> [S]cripture makes two sorts of conversion: one Passive, when man is converted by God. In this, man is but a subject, to receive the impression of grace, and no agent at all. For in the creating, setting, or imprinting of righteousnesse, and holinesse in the heart, Will can doe nothing. The second conversion, is *Active*, whereby man beeing converted by God, doth further turn & convert himselfe to God, in all his thoughts, words, & deeds. This conversion is not onely of grace, nor onely of will; but partly of grace, and partly of will: yet so as grace is the principall agent, & will but the instrument of grace.[2]

As Perkins indicates, prevenient grace can neither be earned nor successfully sought, but once given it frees the recipient to choose whether to cooperate with subsequent grace. In restoring the possibility of choice, however, it also gives Satan the opportunity to win converts to his cause, for though he cannot intercept the original dispensation, he may through temptation divert the human will from collaborating in its own conversion. Thus a corollary to Luther's doctrine of justification is the ethics of intention. If faith rather than works is the basis of redemption, then all external observances lack intrinsic merit. The priority of the spiritual condition over its outward manifestations is the assumption underlying Reformation attacks on prescribed church ritual, and it also forms the basis for Milton's position on divorce, which holds that incompatibility is a more serious breach of marital concord than adultery. Not even ostensibly charitable acts are a certain index to election, but the saved may be distinguished from the unregenerate on the basis of their intentions. "The outward work of love is not sufficient," Calvin declares, "but it is intention that counts."[3]

Acknowledging the importance of intention as the special field of grace's influence, the Elder Brother attributes the Lady's invulnerability not to her chastity but to the humility (431) and sincerity (454) with which she maintains it, and Comus recruits his victims through an assault on their wills. Just as the wand can paralyze the Lady only because she yields control over her body to Comus, so the elixir with which he increases his retinue derives its power from the assent of his victims. Not the potion but the attitude of the taster effects the transformation, "For most do taste," the Attendant Spirit explains, "through fond intemperate thirst" (67). The elixir then is only the occasion, not the cause for Comus's victims to yield to the baser instincts the tempter represents, and its magical power extends only to making the body a true reflection of a mind already bestial in its lack of self-restraint. Drinking is the action which manifests and seals the commitment, but intention is the source of the corruption.

Like the elixir itself, the context in which it is offered confirms the importance of will to the temptation. Because Comus maintains his power only through the complicity of his victims, his trickery cannot extend beyond providing the conditions for the temptation to occur. In his disguise he can induce the Lady to follow him to his palace by pretending he is leading her "to a low / But loyal cottage" (319-320), but once there he has to reveal his deception in order for the temptation to be effective. To persuade her to drink by preying on her ignorance offers Comus no more of a victory than to paralyze her body. His goal is her will, and for him to conquer that, she must realize the source of the gift and assent to what it implies.

In refusing his cup the Lady defines the moral issue as one of intention rather than action. Similarly the ensuing debate turns on Nature's intentions in conferring her gifts. Claiming that Nature intends beauty and pleasure to be indulged, not hoarded, Comus interprets her meaning as a legitimization of appetite, all plenitude and no degree. To the Lady, however, sensory pleasures are the bounty given by a "good cateress" who "Means her provision only to the good / That live according to her sober laws / And holy dictate of spare Temperance" (764-767). The Lady's argument conforms more closely to the position we expect a poem of Milton's to uphold, but the Nature she encounters in the Wood remains ambiguous, capable of admitting either interpretation. In fact, the available evidence seems to support Comus, for if the Lady has her virtue to thank for her present discomfiture, Comus's victims betray no consciousness of loss from their intemperance. Thus while she cannot summon immediate support in favor of the pleasures of restraint, Comus's view is inductive, based on experience. Like appearance, though, experience by itself is often confusing and contradictory, subject to multiple interpretations. Aware that the mind, cut free from the moorings of instruction, tends to find in the external world an image of itself, Milton insisted that a firm anchoring in authority should precede the experience he includes in his program of educational reform. In the masque the Bridgewater estate functions as a symbol for civilization and its nurturing of the mind predisposed to virtue, and as pilgrims from that place where they have been "nurs't in Princely lore" (34), the Lady and her brothers continue to resolve the ambiguities of their present circumstances in the terms their education provides.

If experience is meaningful only when it is placed in an interpretive context, then memory is a faculty crucial to those who seek to resist what Comus offers. For while he maintains control over the wills of his victims by inducing them to forget their previous lives, the Lady exercises her volition partly by activating her memory. Startled by the sound of Comus's revelry, she yields momentarily to fear but regains her emotional equilibrium by recalling her attendants: "Conscience . . . pure-ey'd Faith, white-handed Hope . . . And thou unblemish't form of Chastity" (212-215). The recollection clears her mind "Of calling shapes and beck'ning shadows dire, / And airy tongues that syllable men's names / On Sands and Shores and desert Wildernesses" (207-209). Although memory has provided the opening through which these fantasies invade her mind, her steadfastness is restored because she can also summon memories that reassure. But the overthrow to which her mind will not yield on its own Comus hopes to accomplish through his rhetoric, whose effect is as Lethean as his potion. Like Satan's wooing of Eve, Comus's appeal is *carpe diem*, urging the Lady to accept the present moment without considering past or future; and it is sophistical, based on assumptions about Nature whose dubiousness his suasive power is designed to make the hearer forget. As Augustine explains, however, memory provides the means to transcend the immediate, allowing one to interpret a phenomenon or an event on terms other than those which it supplies.[4] Consequently, in citing philosophy to win the Lady, Comus introduces the means of his refutation, for to her trained mind his words evoke the memory of a Nature better than the one he offers.

Recalling the ideal Nature her authorities teach, the Lady opposes Comus's hedonism with a philosophical defense of temperance, whose sexual form is chastity. Yet as temperance becomes abstinence when she is offered Comus's elixir, so in her argument she turns from chastity to virginity. Virginity may be used here interchangeably with the other two virtues, but it seems to make more sense to regard the alteration in vocabulary as marking the final steps in a process of narrowing and focusing that has begun with the Prologue.[5] From "the starry threshold of *Jove's* Court / . . . where those immortal shapes / Of bright aërial Spirits live inspher'd / In Regions mild of calm and serene Air" (1-4), the Attendant Spirit descends to earth, a smaller and dimmer sphere. As the narrowing progresses, however, the connotations are reversed: within "this pinfold" (7) confinement and seclusion characterize the most praiseworthy inhabitants. Thus we survey earth's expanse, then narrow our focus to one preeminent island, then to one estate of particular distinction. And finally the Lady, who is an emissary from her father's moral oasis, is forced to retreat even from her own body to protect her mind from Comus's assault. Turning in her argument from chastity to virginity, then, the Lady replicates this progression. Like the structure of the masque itself, she moves from outer to inner, from behavior to the intention it expresses.

In refuting the false words of Comus, the Lady discloses the foundation of her virtue in the inner Word. Comus tempts her by an appeal to Nature's laws, and she responds first by answering him on his own terms, arguing that Nature teaches a higher standard than the one he practices. The learned response he evokes, however, is a negative argument based on classical philosophy and assuming an ideal whose verity she cannot demonstrate. Thus paralyzed by his magic she turns to a positive declaration of faith in "the sage / And serious doctrine of Virginity" (786-787), whose "sublime notion and high mystery" (785) Comus cannot follow though he feels its power. In itself, temperance like chastity is a virtue humanly attainable, and as it balances in a reasonable way the claims of the body against those of the spirit, it contemplates the rewards Nature according to the Lady promises to those worthy of them. Yet in order for self-restraint to be redeemed in God's sight, the Christian must be prepared to relinquish the goal, to act in faith without thought of reward.

Because it cannot be earned, virginity can be seen as a metaphor for the Reformation view of faith.[6] It is also an appropriate attribute in the Lady's case because, in her willingness to surrender even the lawful pleasures of the body, she represents the self-denial which to Protestants characterizes faith and precedes all good works. For Calvin self-denial is "the sum of the Christian life." With Romans 12:1 as an authority, he describes self-denial as an emptying of the mind's "carnal sense" in a renewal which presents the believers' "bodies to God as a living sacrifice, holy and acceptable to him."[7] Rejecting "this corporal rind" (664) in favor of her intellectual freedom, then, the Lady clears her mind of its carnality, annihilating all thought of self and yielding entirely to heaven's disposing.

As she attends to the spiritual source of her virtue, the Lady appears to be abandoning along with her body the entire sublunary realm to Comus's governance. Adopting an intellectual posture which Comus translates into a physical condition, she seems to suggest that spiritual innocence can be preserved only at the cost of withdrawing from the world, dedication to eternal truth maintained only by relinquishing temporal pleasures. Her withdrawal extends even to her use of words. Inclined at first not to speak at all, she breaks her silence with a refutation of Comus's lies that lacks the sensuous appeal of her song or the charm of the Elder Brother's philosophy. The harshness of her reply, like the absolute terms of her rejection, invites us to interpret the masque as an affirmation of Neoplatonic dualism, denigrating all things physical and transitory from the perspective of eternity and the spirit. But her position here is not the one with which the masque concludes.

The complicity of the temporal world with Comus's magic makes it indeed a dangerous labyrinth even for God's chosen to traverse, and Milton insists upon the inadequacies of human intellect alone to deal with the illusions it encounters. But the *contemptus mundi* of Neoplatonism is countered by the emphasis in Augustinian Christianity on the material world as the context in which people come to know God. Augustine rejected dualism when he realized that creation by God implies the intrinsic goodness of all things. While with the Fall people became subject to the enslavement of sense and passion, through the Incarnation of the Word they were redeemed, their capacity to use the world for God's glory restored.[8] Despite this recognition, and as the probable result of his strong sexual appetites and his thorough grounding in Platonic philosophy, Augustine remained fearful that the temporal world will lure one away from the concerns of the spirit. Yet his campaigns against various heresies demonstrate his continuing belief that eternal truth is to be realized not simply in transcendent experience but also in human affairs.

Protestants retained Augustine's sense of the priority of the eternal Word, and some of them embraced without qualification the *contemptus mundi* implicit in Platonism. Most, however, perceived the need to advance the cause of reformation through whatever instruments the temporal world provides. Although the ethics of intention has primarily a vertical axis, justifying the human being to God, Protestants quickly became conscious of the solipsistic and antinomian potentials latent in an exclusive reliance upon the inward oracle. Consequently, in order to sustain the reformation as a movement, theologians took care to emphasize the place of works in their schema. Even though works cannot earn salvation, the argument runs, the regenerate will seek to be virtuous spontaneously. Despite his insistence in the *Christian Doctrine* that "It is faith that justifies, and only that which justifies can make any work good," Milton also asserts earlier in the same treatise that "the only living faith is a faith which acts" (CPW, 6: 639, 490). Action then is encouraged and approved; indeed, the true Church requires that its constituents apply themselves to the task of reformation without tarrying. Thus the progressive withdrawal that culminates in the Lady's disclosing the essence of her virtue is followed by a release that allows her to move back into the world where her faith can be realized in action.

Under the pressure of Comus's attentions, the Lady reveals the faith that she maintains through the collaboration of grace and will. But while prevenient grace is necessary to begin the process of sanctification and subsequent grace necessary to persevere in it, the Christian is not fully sanctified until he has received a further blessing, purifying him of the burden of sin. The Attendant Spirit makes the Lady's complete renewal explicit by summoning Sabrina, whose history highlights the significant elements of the Lady's ordeal. Like the Lady, Sabrina has preserved her virtue through self-denial, and heavenly intervention restores to both virgins the possibility of acting in the world. Further, as Sabrina is transformed to a goddess by the application of "Ambrosial Oils" (840), so the sign of the Lady's renewal is the sacramental water of baptism. Although baptism is the ceremony of spiritual purification, Protestants emphasize that the sacraments are the seal of rather than the vehicle for grace. Thus even before Sabrina arrives the Lady has demonstrated her possession of the spiritual gifts baptism represents, but it is nonetheless appropriate that the restoration of her freedom to act is accompanied by a sacramental gesture. For as the baptismal water symbolizes the operation of grace in a temporal instrument, so it seals the reuniting of the Lady's spirit and body, the restored possibility of realizing intention in action. With her will purified through self-denial, the trinity of virtues to which the Lady had originally appealed—Faith, Hope, and Chastity—can issue at last in the acts of charity they all anticipate.

[II]

Persevering in her faith, the Lady responds positively to what Perkins refers to as the "generall calling . . . which is common to all that live in the Church of God."[9] Insofar as her acts are to become truly serviceable, however, they must be both predicated on self-denial and performed in the context of another kind of calling. For Milton as for most Protestants, vocation comprises not just the New Testament call to salvation but the Old Testament call to service.[10] Depending on the number of functions Christians perform in society, they may have several different vocations in the Old Testament sense. To his wife a man has vocational responsibilities as a husband, to his children as a father, to his neighbor as a neighbor. But the most important of these functions, the one commonly designated as a special or personal calling, is the Christian's social vocation, the work performed as a member of the community. Because, as Perkins says, this role is "ordained and imposed on man by God, for the common good," the Christian customarily enjoys divine sanction for actions only in the exercise of its functions.[11] According to Calvin, "each individual has his own kind of living assigned to him by the Lord as a sort of sentry post so that he may not heedlessly wander about through life. Now, so necessary is this distinction that all our actions are judged in his sight by it, often indeed far otherwise than in the judgment of human and philosophical reason."[12]

The particular vocation through which the Lady will perform her charitable actions remains undefined in *Comus*. At least early on in the masque she seems to be incipiently a poet, and the Epilogue suggests as well that she will fulfill an important vocational role in a consecrated marriage. But the Lady is not simply an individual; she is a representative of the audience, and their vocation is an issue implicit in the political event for which the masque was commissioned.

Written to celebrate the investiture of the Earl of Bridgewater as the Lord President of Wales, the masque praises the "tract" newly entrusted to the Earl not as a cloister but as a base of operations from which the "noble Peer" will guide "with temper'd awe . . . / An old and haughty Nation proud in Arms" (30-33). As the Lady's retreat must be succeeded by a return to the world of sensation and appearance, so Lady Alice's father must seek both to preserve his family's nobility and to make it current, to extend its domain. Thus the Lady's transition from the world of the masque to the world of the audience contains a compliment and a prophecy. Politicians whose duties must inevitably raise questions about the relationship between virtue and action, the Lord President and his guests are complimented because, when the children join them, the implication is that the ideal community of saints is identical with the real governing nobles of England. They are encouraged to infer that they have already negotiated the process of purification the Lady undergoes and are thus assured that the acts necessary to their vocation are sanctioned by God. If the Epilogue seems to promise the Lady that her exertions will be rewarded in marriage, however, for the audience its paradisal vision points also to the expected millennium, the transformation of England into a New Jerusalem; their calling is to work toward this end.

Despite the suggestions carried by the end of the masque, Milton in *Comus* is most concerned about the response to the call to salvation, which leads to the purification upon which all worthy action is predicated. In *Paradise Regained*, however, he examines through Christ's trial the answer to the call to service and the discovery of a language through which that service is to be realized. Although in time and in style there is a large distance between the masque and the brief epic, they are similar in the apparent asceticism their protagonists uphold. But while the Lady's motives and actions are purified through a process that the masque traces, the Son is assumed to be already pure. John Hill has argued that Christ in his trial perfects the self-denial essential to the practice of his vocation, but though baptism is the climax of the plot in *Comus*, in *Paradise Regained* it initiates the action.[13] And Christ submits to the baptism itself "Not thence to be more pure, but to receive / The testimony of Heaven" (I.77-78). Satan's offers, then, do not elicit self-denial in the way Comus's attentions do from the Lady; rather, they provide the Son the opportunity to demonstrate a perfection already complete. As we discover in Book I, he has previously dismissed most of the possibilities Satan invites him to seize, and consequently the temptations lack even the degree of tension and drama we find in the masque. Yet the exchange between the Son and his tempter is more than just a ritualistic exercise.

Before the Fall Adam learns through a dialectic between external and internal revelation, but thereafter, Milton suggests in *Areopagitica*, we come to know good only in constrast to its opposite (CPW, 2: 514). As he resists the false words of Satan, then, Christ comes to appreciate more fully the nature of his divine call. In the process of being tempted, Christ fulfills the roles of prophet, king, and priest, but he realizes these aspects of the Messianic task through the ministry he will undertake immediately upon leaving the wilderness.[14] Although he is resolved "By winning words to conquer willing hearts, / And make persuasion do the work of fear" (I.222-223), however, he must first discover the means to convey his message. God sends the Son into the desert so that he may foil "the Tempter. . . / In all his wiles" (I.5-6). Obediently withstanding temptation, Christ will recover what Adam lost through disobedience. Yet the point of Milton's treatment is not simply that Satan's weapons will prove ineffectual but that through the Son they will be redeemed for divine purposes. Thus as in the war in heaven the battle which Christ and Satan join in the wilderness is one of words. At the same time that he rejects what Satan offers, Christ also redefines Satan's terms, purifying them of demonic connotation and making them serviceable to his ministry. And his defeat of Satan becomes complete when he fully realizes the significance of himself as the Incarnate Word, a paradox whose mystery overcomes Satan even as it restores to language the possibility of expressing divinity.

The Son becomes aware of his particular calling through Mary's description of the circumstances surrounding his birth, and he finds her assessment confirmed in Scriptures. Yet even before he can give a specific name to his aspirations, he has already been preparing for the role of Messiah, choosing how best "to promote all truth, / All righteous things" (I.205-206). He has immersed himself in the Law, and before he opts for teaching, he considers the career of a military conqueror:

> . . . one while
> To rescue *Israel* from the *Roman* yoke,
> Then to subdue and quell o'er all the earth

    Brute violence and proud Tyrannic pow'r,
    Till truth were freed, and equity restor'd.   (I.216-220)

Just as the Lady must preserve her beauty and innocence for a consecrated marriage, so Christ must also be a good steward, husbanding God's gifts until he can employ them in his divine mission.[15]

The preservation and development of one's innate qualities, however, is not in itself a positively worthy action in God's sight. We must prepare ourselves to perform our appointed work, but the burden of making our labors serviceable rests with God. As Luther advises, "we ought to labor, but not to prescribe the end and outcome of our work."[16] Thus while truly good actions occur customarily within one's vocation, the calling itself does not guarantee a positive warrant to all vocational acts. Although Perkins insists that "untill a mans person please God, his worke shall never please him," he also maintains that to be genuinely holy works require "a double Sanctification. The first of the worker; the second, of the worke and action to be done."[17] And because the sanction for works is initiated by God, we must await what Luther calls the "definite hour," the time appointed for their fruition:

> All human works and efforts have a certain and definite time of acting, of beginning, and of ending, beyond human control. . . . It is not up to us to prescribe the time, the manner, or the effect of things that are to be done; and so it is obvious that here our strivings and efforts are unreliable. . . . it is useless for men to be tormented by their strivings . . . they do not accomplish anything, even though they were to burst, unless the proper time and the hour appointed by God has come.[18]

The Lady, then, must accept her paralysis "while Heav'n sees good" (665), and Christ, despite his certainty that he is the Messiah whom the prophets foretell, must await "The time prefixt" (I.269) to begin his ministry. While their intentions are pure and their stewardship faithful, they must stand and wait until God chooses to employ them.

Under most circumstances Christians are called to the ordinary offices of society, sacred and secular. When the situation is
urgent, however, God may summon his special servants through
an "extraordinary calling," which according to Perkins is issued
only in two cases: first, "in the founding and planting of the
Church," and second, "when the Church of God is defaced, and
universall Apostasie taketh place."[19] For the second category
Perkins has in mind the Reformation, and he cites Luther as an
example of one who has received an extraordinary call. The
apostles are instances of the first category, but for Milton so is
Christ, who receives his call in all three of the ways Perkins lists
as the means for extraordinary calling to be communicated.
Christ hears the call in its first form, by God's "own immediate voice,"
at the baptism; in the second, "by the ministry of creatures," through
the proclamation of John as well as through the evidence Mary
provides; and in the third, "by speciall instinct, and extraordinary
inspiration of the spirit," when the Spirit of God descends and leads
him "by some strong motion" (I.290) into the wilderness.[20]

The call that leads the Son into the desert is not merely
initiatory; it is perpetual, and he must remain attentive to its
guidance if he is to execute his vocation faithfully. In his treatise
on self-denial, the preacher Christopher Wilson advises that
good actions can be neither negligent nor rash.[21] Ignoring the
proscription against eating the fruit, Adam and Eve fail in their
respective vocations through negligence. Christ on the other
hand is tempted repeatedly to rashness, not so much to abandon
his vocation as to arrogate to himself decisions about the sched-
ule for the performance of his appointed task and the means of its
accomplishment. In effect, the Son is invited to rely on himself
rather than on God for the success of his mission, and to accept
Satan as a guide preferable to the Holy Spirit. But as Thomas
Taylor reminds his readers in his commentary on the temptations, we must examine our motives in order to make certain all
consideration of self has been expunged:

> Those that are led by Gods spirit, whatsoever they be about,
> they will looke to the motion, what warrant they have for it,
> whence it is, and whether it tends, whether they be led, or

undertake things of their owne head: they looke whether the thing be good in it selfe, whether good in them, whether convenient in circumstances, whether it belong unto them: and hence they do it chearfully, and with a blessing on it. Whereas whom Satan caries, they looke for no warrant, they set themselves on worke, and execute their owne lusts, humours, and desires; . . . and therefore, if it be in any thing that is good, every thing is begun as with a left hand, they are without blessing and protection.[22]

Satan frequently invites the Son to perform actions that seem in themselves blameless or even laudable, and Christ in many cases will later do what here he refuses. Under the present circumstances, however, he cannot accept the legitimacy of these actions because Satan urges them in a context that makes the motives suspect, hoping to diminish the influence of the inner Word by awakening Christ's self-interest.

In the second temptation Satan will appeal to Christ's patriotism, claiming that "Zeal and Duty" (III.172) require him to take the readiest way to David's throne; and to his political idealism, urging him to purify Rome of its corruption. While these motives are in themselves praiseworthy, Satan taints them not only with his own covert purposes but with the fringe benefits of worldly fame and power. Similarly in the first temptation Satan invites Christ to work a miracle that will serve apparently good ends but that in the present context is inseparable from motives of self-interest which Christ must abjure. Urging him to turn stones to bread, Satan offers a practical justification: "So shalt thou save thyself and us relieve / With Food, whereof we wretched seldom taste" (I.344-345). Christ in his ministry will violate the law in the name of self-preservation (Mt. 12:1-9), and he everywhere enjoins service to one's neighbor. In this instance, however, he refuses because he perceives the challenge implicit in Satan's suggestion. To perform a miracle here would be to indulge the natural desire to establish his identity in the face of Satan's feigned skepticism: "if thou be the Son of God" (I.342). But more important, by acting to provide food for himself, Christ would be distrusting God's providence, relying on his own powers rather than on God's to deliver him.

Christ does not simply dismiss Satan's temptation; he also redefines the nature of sustenance in a way which will allow him to reclaim as instruments of his ministry actions and objects he refuses as essential in themselves. Instead of bread as the source of physical nourishment, Christ offers the Word of God as the staff of spiritual life. The association of Word and food runs throughout the first temptation.[23] Christ links "each Word / Proceeding from the mouth of God" (I.349-350) with manna, and he cites the fasts of Moses and Elijah to show that physical food is not necessary when God provides nourishment. Further, in denouncing the false oracles he declares to Satan, "lying is thy sustenance, thy food" (I.429). The Word Christ refers to in his original rejection is the Scriptures, and to Perkins this appeal demonstrates "that the *written word of God*, rightly welded by the hand of faith, is the most sufficient weapon for the repelling of Satan and the vanquishing him in all his temptations."[24] In Milton's elaboration of the dialogue with Satan, however, Christ comes to recognize that the "living Oracle" and the "inward Oracle" (I.460, 463) are equally important manifestations of God's Word, and by silencing the oracles through which Satan deludes the Gentiles, the Son acknowledges that he is called to be the true prophet. Yet though he redeems this oracular function by relocating its source not in Satan but in God, the most important possibility latent in the first temptation must await his ministry for fruition. As Christ in order to establish the authority of his teaching will later work miracles similar to the one he refuses to perform in self-vindication or self-reliance, so the physical bread he rejects as necessary in itself he will later reclaim as a symbol for the nourishment he offers, both in feeding the multitude and in initiating the Eucharist.

Although the first temptation has no point of reference except for the present circumstances in which Christ finds himself, the terms of his refusal suggest the means for his further trial. By appealing to Scripture to reject Satan's urging, Christ establishes an apparent reliance that Satan will test, first with regard to the Law, then to the Prophets. The banquet scene both extends the first temptation, making food its object, and introduces the second, the "Table richly spread, in regal mode"

(II.340) looking forward to the opulence of the kingdoms Christ will be offered. But its primary significance, it seems to me, lies in the attitude toward the Law Christ is invited to adopt, and the relevance of this attitude to his ministry. Despite Satan's assurances, the feast does contain food forbidden by Hebraic dietary laws.[25] The dilemma in which the Son is thus placed is typical of Satan's insidious methods. For if Christ refuses the banquet by invoking the Law, he is accepting its authority, while if he acts with apparent disregard for it, he is arrogating to himself the authority to cancel its ritual proscriptions. In his ministry Christ will gather food on the Sabbath and, scandalizing the devout Jews, attend a feast given by a tax collector. Here, however, he fulfills the Law by intensifying its rigors, refusing like the Lady in *Comus* not the gift but the giver.

What he may do in the performance of his vocation is presumption if undertaken before his mission is fully defined, before he receives the divine warrant for action. Thus if one aspect of the temptation is to adhere literally to the Hebraic ceremonial laws, another is to accept from Satan the literal fulfillment of his mission, to raise Eden "in the waste Wilderness" (I.7). The "pleasant Grove" (II.289) to which the Son is enticed recreates, like Spenser's Bower of Bliss, a false paradise. By making available through art devoid of spirit all the sensory delights of the original Eden, Satan invites Christ to accept civilization as an adequate replacement for the Garden, urbane indulgence as the exact counterpart to innocence. But the decadence and excess of the banquet, despite Satan's claim to tempt Christ "to satisfy / Lawful desires of Nature, not beyond" (II.229-230), make it repugnant and offer Christ an example of what the new Eden cannot be. For Christ as for the Lady, sensory pleasure can be innocently enjoyed only when the agents of delight are used purely, according to God's intentions.

If Christ cannot be tricked into either submitting to the Law or prematurely declaring it abrogated, Satan hopes to tempt him with the Kingdom to which the Prophets entitle him. But as he refuses to take a material paradise in recompense for the one that has been lost, so he will refuse to accept a literal throne in satisfaction of his mission. Rather, in rejecting Satan's offers he appropriates the vocabulary for his own future use, redefining the nature of kingship and redirecting the chiliastic expectations the Messianic prophecies evoke from the Hebrews. The introductory scenes of Book II anticipate this movement, for while Andrew, Simon, and Mary all continue to define the Messiah in political and military terms, by arriving through consternation at patient acceptance, they show that they are already in possession of the Kingdom Christ in fact comes to inaugurate.

What is incipient at the beginning of Book II is manifest at its conclusion, where Christ's response to the first of the kingdom temptations contains the substance of his method with all the rest. Assuming that the Son's abstinence from the banquet is due to his greater aspirations, Satan first offers not a kingdom but the means to acquire it for himself. But although he cites examples to disprove Satan's contention that riches are necessary, the primary ground for Christ's rejection is his introduction of a new concept of kingship. In the first place he circumscribes the extent of reign, narrowing it from rule over others to self-rule. But he also redefines the nature of kingly behavior, seeing it not as commanding his constituency but as serving them: "For therein stands the office of a King, / His Honor, Virtue, Merit, and chief Praise, / That for the Public all this weight he bears" (II.463-465). The concept of king as servant, which Christ will manifest in his ministry and his sacrifice, is reiterated and elaborated upon in the terms of his final rejection, in which he insists that "to give a Kingdom hath been thought / Greater and nobler done, and to lay down / Far more magnanimous than to assume" (II.481-483). In the sense of "give up," this passage describes what the Son has already performed, voluntarily surrendering his heavenly throne for, as Milton puts it in the Nativity Ode, "a darksome House of mortal Clay" (14). But in the sense of "confer," the lines point to the universal kingdom it is his mission to offer humanity, the kingdom in which Andrew, Simon, and Mary have already become subjects. Christ has come not simply to be a king but to make available to all people the kingdom he possesses.

The later kingdom temptations provide Christ the opportunity to pursue some of the implications contained in his answer to the first. Offered wealth as a means to kingdom, he rejects Satan's premises and redefines kingship, calling self-rule the most important exercise of authority and finding regality not in opulence but in charity. Similarly, when he is offered a throne as the means to glory, he both condemns Satan's concept of the term and offers his own. Glory as Satan intends it is merely "the blaze of fame, / The people's praise . . . / And what the people but a herd confus'd, / A miscellaneous rabble, who extol / Things vulgar, and well weigh'd, scarce worth the praise?" (III.47-51). But there is as well a true fame, typified by Job and described also in "Lycidas," that is achieved "when God / . . . with approbation marks / The just man, and divulges him through Heaven / To all his Angels, who with true applause / Recount his praises" (III.60-64).

The same formula of rejection and redefinition applies also to the last temptation of Book III, the offer of Parthia's military might as a means to secure David's throne. The Son's response denigrates the "Luggage of war" as an "argument / Of human weakness rather than of strength" (III.401-402). But if the reliance on physical strength implies weakness, there is, as Christ has earlier pointed out, an apparent weakness which is strength. Anticipating the trials his Sonship will entail, he observes, "who best / Can suffer, best can do; best reign, who first / Well hath obey'd" (III.194-196). Although he may not yet fully understand it, Christ's axiom is applicable not only to the future pains he knows he must endure but also to his present circumstances. Just as he silences the oracles by proclamation, so here saying is equivalent to doing. His submission to the necessity of Satan's harassment fits him for rule even as he rejects the kingdoms Satan offers. And as the closing lines of Book III indicate, he is winning a spiritual battle even as he rejects the means of military conquest: "So spake *Israel's* true King, and to the Fiend / Made answer meet, that made void all his wiles. / So fares it when with truth falsehood contends" (III.441-443).

Although Christ begins his rejection of kingdom by apparently limiting the concept of governance to self-rule, in the course of redefining kingship he discloses a universality to his role that both provides Satan the opportunity for further trial and contributes to his increasing perplexity. In refusing Satan's offer of Parthian military aid, Christ seems to betray aspirations that extend beyond the bounds of the Hebrew nation. As he will later denounce the Romans for their inward slavery, so he asks why he should trouble himself to free from political captivity a people who submit willingly to spiritual bondage:

> Should I of these the liberty regard,
> Who freed, as to their ancient Patrimony,
> Unhumbl'd, unrepentant, unreform'd,
> Headlong would follow, and to thir Gods perhaps
> Of *Bethel* and of *Dan?* No, let them serve
> Thir enemies, who serve Idols with God.   (III.427-432)

Interpreting this denunciation as an escalation in Christ's goals, Satan offers him first Rome, with its "wide domain / . . . ample Territory, wealth and power, / Civility of Manners, Arts, and Arms, / And long Renown" (IV.81-84); and then Athens, through whose learning Christ may "let extend [his] mind o'er all the world" (IV.223). But though Christ appears to be abandoning the Scriptural prophecies by denigrating the literal throne of David, in rejecting the conditions Satan places on the offer of Rome he reverts as in the first temptation to a biblical injunction: "It is written / The first of all Commandments, Thou shalt worship / The Lord thy God" (IV.175-177). And in refusing the learning Athens represents, he redefines wisdom, locating it in the inspiration the Scriptures reflect.

The relationship of Christ to the Scriptures is an issue in all the temptations. In the first he acknowledges Scriptures as the Word of God, but in silencing the oracles he recognizes the importance as well of his own teaching and of the inner Word, whose priority Milton asserts in the *Christian Doctrine* (CPW, 6: 587-590). Through the second and third books he averts the trap of the Law Satan has set for him and then reinterprets the prophecies which foretell a kingly Messiah. The problem is raised with the greatest urgency, however, in the last group, beginning with the offer of wisdom and concluding with the temptation of the pinnacle.

Like the offer of temporal thrones, the temptation to wisdom is grounded in prophecy. The forecasts of Simeon and Anna, to which Mary refers earlier, both stress the role of the Messiah as a wise man, and Satan finds in Christ's youthful attraction to the temple the basis for his apparent indifference to worldly kingdoms. Yet like the other temptations, this one is tainted by the suspect motives which Satan attaches to the offer. For Christ is invited to receive wisdom not as a good in itself but only as a way to achieve fame. Richard Baxter makes "*the Reputation of Wisdom and Learning*" a part of the vainglory that must be rejected for self-denial to be complete:

> The things themselves are very excellent, and to be desired and much sought after: but not for our own Honour, but the Service and Honour of the Lord. . . . This part of *self-denial* consisteth not in a contempt of Learning or Wisdom, nor in a neglect of it: for this were a sin: but in a neglect of *self* that would make an advantage of it, for its own carnal exaltation; and in a contempt of the Honour and vainglory which may redound by it to our selves, further then such honour is serviceable to God.[26]

It is then in part the self-aggrandizing aspect of the temptation that Christ rejects, and his equivocal answer suggests his unwillingness to claim for himself what his frequent references to classical literature and history have shown he already knows: "Think not but that I know these things; or think / I know them not" (IV.286-287).

Motive aside, Satan makes a persuasive case for Christ's need to rely on pagan philosophy in his ministry, and Christ's categorical denial seems, like the Lady's abjuring her "corporal rind," to exceed the demands of the occasion. But the question is really one of priority, of distinguishing what is essential from what is merely useful. Howard Schultz has demonstrated how Christ's rejection resonates with the "learned-ministry" debate, in which Milton had argued for piety rather than a university degree as the one necessary criterion for a pulpit.[27] Reflecting the informing Word of God only with distortion, Greek philosophy can offer nothing essential to salvation, and the ornaments of pagan poetry and oratory, because they are not grounded in revealed truth, are similarly hollow when compared "With *Sion's* songs, to all true tastes excelling, / Where God is prais'd aright, and Godlike men, / The Holiest of Holies, and his Saints" (IV.347-349). As Paul shows, a knowledge of Greek philosophy can be useful, but since it is a part of Christ's mission to introduce a new way of thinking and speaking about God, to translate his message exclusively into terms his audience finds familiar would be to defeat his purposes.

Calvin, Edward Dowey points out, "favored the use in preaching (Commentary on Acts 14 and 17) and writing (I.v) of an enlightened view of the revelation in Creation. He did not care whether the enlightenment came from Cicero or Plato or Aratus for use against 'gentile' polytheism and idolatry, or from the psalms and prophets for use against the errors of the 'papists.' "[28] The Lady employs classical learning in this negative way, opposing Comus first by an appeal to an ethic based on Nature, and Satan likewise observes that "Error by his own arms is best evinc't" (IV.235). The point, however, is not simply to refute false claims but to establish truth. As the Lady's appeal to virginity makes clear, then, her reliance on pagan philosophy "is not a bridge to true faith, but a battering ram against false 'faiths.' . . . Then, after this clearing away of the bad, the gospel is to be preached."[29] Rejecting as necessary the poetry, philosophy, and rhetoric of ancient Greece, Christ and his ministers are thus free to use them wherever they can be appropriately employed in the service of revealed truth.

If Greek philosophy is not essential to the dissemination of Christ's message, then natural signs after the Fall are an even less certain guide to truth. As the Lady's debate with Comus has shown, Nature tends to yield the meaning its interpreter wishes to assign to it. In the storm Satan attempts not only to frighten Christ but also to induce him to accept divination for divine prophecy, his reading of the Book of Nature for the Word of God.[30] The tempest, he tells the Son, is evidence of God's displeasure, and as a result of Christ's passivity he will have to endure "Sorrows and labors, opposition, hate, / . . . scorns, reproaches, injuries, / Violence and stripes, and lastly cruel death" (IV.386-388). While the violence of the storm makes Satan's reading plausible, the night ends with a dawn that seems to suggest an alternative possibility:

Thus pass'd the night so foul till morning fair
Came forth with Pilgrim steps in amice gray;
Who with her radiant finger still'd the roar
Of thunder, chas'd the clouds, and laid the winds,
And grisly Specters, which the Fiend had rais'd
To tempt the Son of God with terrors dire.   (IV.426-431)

The description seems almost an allegory of the Son's conquest over Satan, but unlike the Lady and in contrast to his previous responses, Christ does not offer to reinterpret Satan's evidence. From the Scriptures he has already learned that his "way must lie / Through many a hard assay even to the death" (I.263-264), but the natural signs Satan reads as threatening punishment Christ denounces "As false portents, not sent from God, but thee" (IV.491).

God of course uses natural signs on occasion to help convey his message, for instance Noah's rainbow and the dove at Christ's baptism. But while they are useful reinforcements to revelation, these visual signs do not themselves impart knowledge of God. Like the elements in the Calvinist view of the sacraments, physical signs may function "as a seal to the word to draw attention to the importance and truth of what is being said," but it is the explicating word that lends the sign its meaning.[31] Unable to comprehend God's proclamation, Satan remains puzzled by the dove, wondering "whate'er it meant" (I.83). Christ on the other hand is not limited by his opponent's literalism. He reduces the sign to a similitude: "The Spirit descended on me like a Dove" (I.282); and when the report reaches Mary, there is no reference to the dove but only to the verbal acknowledgements of John and the Father. Imitating God's method at the baptism, Satan alternates in his temptations between the abstract and the concrete, between verbal offer and visual reinforcement. Christ refuses the temptations because Satan's false words do not evoke the confirmation of the inward oracle, yet they are useful. For Satan is not the author but only the usurper of what he purveys, and thus he cannot limit their potential to his own intentions in offering them. Consequently, as he rejects Satan's invitations, Christ finds progressively disclosed the nature of his ministry and the vocabulary he will employ to convey his message. Although he has found the means to reclaim the terms of previous temptations, Christ has not come to restore the external Eden, in which natural signs were a reliable index to divine meaning, and he therefore ignores the opportunity to place a different construction on the evidence Satan uses to support his soothsaying. In the last of the temptations, however, Satan devises a trap that unintentionally functions as a symbol for Christ's mission, and in realizing its significance, the Son finds his vocation fully defined, the means of its execution provided.

Extending the violence of the storm scene, Satan peremptorily sets Christ on the pinnacle to the temple in what most scholars see as an anticipation of the Cross.[32] Yet it is not Christ's sacrifice but the "glorious work" (IV.634) of his ministry to which the temptations primarily look forward, and the figure of himself standing on the temple functions as a symbol, aiding Christ in defining his relationship to what the temple represents. From their first encounter, Satan's attempts to discover the Son's identity have left Satan uncertain whether he will limit himself to the Hebraic concept of the Messiah or whether his advent is to nullify God's written word. To the Hebrews the temple at Jerusalem is the symbol of their identity as God's chosen people, for it contains the Ark of the Covenant. The commentators interpret the Ark as a type of Christ, partly because its conquest of Dagon seems to prefigure Christ's silencing the oracles. The conforming minister Andrew Willet, for instance, points out, "for as the Arke here, which was the seate of the God of Israel, vanquisheth Dagon: so after that Christ the true light of the world was come, the oracles of Apollo, and other heathen Idols ceased."[33] Thus standing on the temple, Christ becomes a living symbol of his ministry. The figure indicates that his relationship to the Law and the Prophets is not simply literal, obeying their restrictions, nor negative, canceling their effect. Rather he is to fulfill them, completing their design by reinterpreting the terms in which they describe his mission. His position on the temple, then, defines his relationship to the Hebraic culture much as the sculpture on Chartres cathedral, in which the Apostles are depicted standing on the heads of the Prophets, indicates the relationship between the Old and New Testaments.

The meaning of the symbol Satan unwittingly constructs is replicated in Christ's decisive final answer. As he has previously redefined the terms of Satan's offers, here he provides an illuminating new perspective on Scripture itself. When Satan suggests that he cast himself down from the temple, Christ responds to Satan's use of biblical prophecy with an appeal to Law: "Also it is written, / Tempt not the Lord thy God" (IV.560-561). Although he has previously praised the Scriptures for their clarity, his quotation of the biblical injunction assumes a double meaning in this context, for the Lord, he and Satan now realize, is not simply God the Father but also the Son. Christ's application of this title to himself indicates that he now feels the divine warrant for action that he has been awaiting, but it also reveals his arrival at a language that is at last fully adequate to his ministry. Stanley Fish argues that in this scene Christ works "a linguistic miracle in which language, the primary sign of personality, becomes the means by which personality is extinguished. The Son performs the impossible feat of saying silence and makes himself disappear."[34] On the contrary, it seems to me that Christ's victory over Satan is the result of his discovering a medium that speaks not silence but himself. In his rebellion Satan has invented the possibility that words may be detached not only from their referents but also from the mind it is their original function to express. Here, however, Christ restores the expressive capacity of language, for he devises a medium through whose doubleness he can reveal the mystery of his own nature.

Even Baxter, who had denounced the rhetorical excesses of Lancelot Andrewes's sermons, recognizes the need to "distinguish between Jesuitical dissembling Equivocation, and the *laudable yea necessary use of Equivocal words, when either the transcendencie of the matter*, the incapacity of men, the paucity of terms, the custom of speech, &c. *hath made them fit or needfull*."[35] Thus Christ in his final reply completes the task of reclaiming what Satan offers by redefining it, and as he assumes his vocational duties he is in full possession of an instrument capable, in the way Baxter suggests, of indicating the miraculous nature of his message. For despite their use of the common idiom of those to whom he preaches, his responses to questions are often cryptic, his parables themselves a means of communicating indirectly what cannot be adequately conveyed in discursive language.

If Milton's brief epic traces Christ's discovery of a language appropriate to his vocation, the style of the poem itself seems to be an exercise in narrative self-denial. The first lines, echoing Virgil's reflection on his pastoral apprenticeship as he begins the *Aeneid*, suggest that the story of Christ's temptation in the wilderness is the true epic subject for which the account of "the happy Garden" (I.1) is only the necessary bucolic prelude. Yet its style does not rival that of *Paradise Lost* but instead seems only to continue the chastened, quiescent tone of the last books without the dramatic necessity imposed upon Michael. Marjorie Nicolson suggests that Milton was imitating the style of the Synoptic Gospels, while Louis Martz and Barbara Lewalski, though they disagree on which genre Milton is using, find the restrained style to be the result of his preserving generic decorum.[36]

Considerations of genre are of course important, but none of these positions explains why the prologue should deliberately evoke expectations that are left unfulfilled. For Fish this misleading beginning initiates a pattern which points to the poem's ethical values, promoting inaction as it celebrates "deeds / Above Heroic" (I.14-15).[37] But the device, like the muted style itself, also calls attention to the fact that the narrator is stepping aside in deference to the central figure. Thus the richness and complexity which we have come to expect from Milton's epic voice are transferred to the Incarnate Word, and as his paradoxical nature eludes Satan and finally defeats him, so the language of poetry itself is redeemed in the double meaning contained in his response to Satan's last temptation. Christ's example does not deny action; rather, like the Lady in *Comus*, he practices the discipline upon which truly worthy action is predicated.

Similarly the restrained verse of *Paradise Regained*, transparently revealing the mystery of the Incarnate Word, does not reject the more elaborate style of *Paradise Lost* so much as it points to the terms on which that style is available, the means by which it is sanctioned.

CHAPTER FIVE

Responding to the Word

❦

The Narrator in Paradise Lost

THE positive response to the call to salvation, which Milton explores in *Comus*, is the prerequisite for the effective performance of one's special vocation, the call to service he examines more thoroughly in *Paradise Regained*. Like the Lady and Christ, the narrator of *Paradise Lost* confronts a world defined by fallen speech, and if the other two protagonists represent stages preparatory to the redemption of language, the epic voice embodies the fulfillment of that process. No less than the ministry for which Christ is preparing, poetry is a divinely appointed vocation, and in order to be "true" it must first be the product of an author who is pure. Particularly in the early verse, Milton stresses the need for the poet to be virtuous, and in the prose he seeks to disarm attacks on his character by arguing that his poetic aspirations preclude the behavior of which he is accused. But in order for his art to be genuinely worthy in God's sight, the poet must also receive a warrant for action in the form of inspiration, the inward vision for which the narrator in *Paradise Lost* repeatedly prays.

Although the epic voice cannot perform his task without divine assistance, the heavenly muse does not reduce her servant to an amanuensis. Rather she permits him access to the principles of God's creation so that he may continue in human words the revelation God accomplishes through the Word. The idea that underlies the physical universe is succinctly stated in the heavenly colloquy, but its manifestation, as Raphael's account shows, is frequently complex, various, indirect. In his parody of divine Creation, Satan appropriates its complexity and obliquity to serve the purposes of deception, but Milton's narrator returns these characteristics to their original function. Through heavenly inspiration the poet's art is redeemed, the full resources of language enlisted in the ongoing revelation of divine beneficence.

[I]

Like Luther and Calvin on works in general, Milton, when he discusses poetry, tends to collapse the distance between the artist and the art. Although he excuses his admiration for "the smooth Elegiack Poets" he had studied in school by distinguishing between aesthetic and moral judgments, he gradually transforms his statement, first blurring and finally erasing the original distinction. While he admits to finding the classical love poets pleasing, he quickly asserts his preference for Dante and Petrarch, "the two famous renowners of *Beatrice* and *Laura* who never write but honour of them to whom they devote their verse, displaying sublime and pure thoughts, without transgression." Relocating the basis of his judgment from technical proficiency to the thoughts expressed, Milton then concludes with another shift, this time attributing the quality of the poet's verse not just to the thoughts he articulates but to his character: "he who would not be frustrate of his hope to write well hereafter in laudable things, ought him selfe to bee a true Poem, that is, a composition, and patterne of the best and honourablest things; not presuming to sing high praises of heroick men, or famous Cities, unlesse he have in himselfe the experience and the practice of all that which is praise-worthy" (*Smec*; CPW, 1: 889-890).

The identification of good poets as good people is of course an ancient idea, occurring as early as Plato and reiterated by the Roman orators, but it is appropriated early by Christianity and given additional support in Protestant theology. Christian writers often employed the concept to demonstrate the inferiority of its originators, for if the Christian religion is better than the pagan, then Christian art must also be superior. Following Augustine, who defended the literary quality of the Bible against its Greek and Roman rivals, Milton in *The Reason of Church Government* bases his hope to surpass "what the greatest and choycest wits of *Athens*, *Rome*, or modern *Italy*, and those Hebrews of old did for their country" not on his skill but on his Christianity (CPW, 1: 812). With the Reformation the idea was further dignified through association with its doctrinal parallel, the ethics of intention. For poetry as for all action according to Luther, "it is always necessary that the substance or person himself be good before there can be any good works, and that good works follow and proceed from the good person."[1]

Especially in his early writing, Milton describes his preparation for the vocation of poetry in terms drawn mainly from classical literature. Pursuing the ideal of making himself a true poem, he immersed himself in a demanding program of study and presented himself as following an ascetic discipline. He wrote Elegy VI, he says, on "an empty stomach" (1) because the singer of sacred songs must live sparingly, subsisting on a diet of herbs and water; and further, "his youth must be innocent of crime and chaste" (63). As it does with the Lady, chastity seems frequently to serve for Milton as a symbol for the spiritual purity that characterizes the Christian life, but it is not the virtue so much as the relationship of his behavior to the inspiration he desires that places his theory in the context of Protestant thought.[2] For while the classical poet may in some sense earn the muse's favor, the regimen Milton undertakes cannot in itself guarantee that his ambitions will be fulfilled. Christ and the Lady, despite the purity the former exhibits and the latter achieves, must await divine sanction before assuming their appointed roles. Similarly the epic voice, while he cultivates "th'upright heart and pure" (I.18) and aspires to perform a task for which he has been "long choosing" (IX.26), recognizes that neither his virtues nor his diligence alone can assure the success of his enterprise. According to the myth of its own creation, the poem is "unpremeditated" (IX.24), the credit for its accomplishment due not to its author's efforts but to the inexplicable attentions of a "Celestial Patroness" (IX.21). Nonetheless the poet submits to the rigors of his program for two reasons: first, to cultivate the eloquence of example, which to Augustine is an essential element of all truly good speech; and second, to purify himself as an appropriate instrument should God choose to employ him.

According to Augustine the speaker must seek to be virtuous first of all in order to gain a hearing: "the life of the speaker has greater weight in determining whether he is obediently heard than any grandness of eloquence."[3] But if his life is to be an instrument of his message, he must not simply be virtuous; he must appear as virtuous as he is. In one sense all Christians are constantly witnessing for Christ, and thus their deeds like those of preachers and divine poets are subject to rhetorical consider-ations. Augustine praises his mother for surrendering her custom of bringing food and wine to the saints' chapels, a practice she abandoned not because her use was intemperate but "so that drunkards should not be given an occasion for excess and also because this kind of anniversary funeral feast is very much like the superstitious ceremony of the pagans."[4] A duty enjoined upon all Christians, however, is a matter of particular urgency for those who bring God's message. As a result of their special authority their lives are subject to constant scrutiny, and so they must weigh their actions as well as their words with utmost care.

Like the feature of Augustine's thought that J. A. Mazzeo calls the rhetoric of silence, the eloquence of example reveals a persistent tendency in Augustine to depreciate the external, spoken words in favor of the silent inner Word, and the influence of this tendency continued into the Reformation. Yet as Mazzeo notes, Augustine was no gnostic, and the rhetoric of silence supports a method of Scriptural exegesis which paradoxically "encouraged greater clarity on the one hand and long flights of symbolic interpretation of the things mentioned in Scripture on the other, flights which obscured any immediacy of perception."[5] Similarly most Protestant theologians, despite their insistence that the speaker's words are hollow unless he is himself pure, nonetheless looked to the words as well as the life, which hypoc-risy may disguise or, in the case of printed texts, distance render inaccessible. Perkins sees the minister's own virtues as most

important to "the simple people," who "behold not the minis-
terie, but the person of the Minister."[6] Calvin, attempting to
define the fruits by which false prophets are distinguished from
true, is even less willing to rely on the speaker's life as an index to
the soundness of the teaching:

> Those who confine them [i.e., the fruits of the teaching] to
> the life are, in my opinion, mistaken. . . . hypocrisy, I do
> own, is at length discovered; for nothing is more difficult
> than to counterfeit virtue. But Christ did not intend to
> submit his doctrine to a decision so unjust in itself, and so
> liable to be misunderstood, as to have it estimated by the life
> of men. Under the *fruits* the *manner of teaching* is itself in-
> cluded, and indeed holds the chief place: for Christ proves
> that he was sent by God from this consideration, that "he
> seeketh not his own glory, but the glory of the Father who
> sent him."[7]

Similarly Baxter, his distrust of rhetoric notwithstanding, looks
not to the life to judge the speech, but to the speech in order to
determine the character of the speaker. "A New heart," he
declares, "will have a New tongue. The fruit of it will appear in
the scope of a mans discourse. . . . though words may be coun-
terfeit, yet true Conversion doth alway change the speech, and
make the tongue also serviceable to those higher Ends, which the
heart is newly set upon. He that before had no mind to speak of
any thing but earthly and fleshly matters, he is now enquiring
after other matters."[8]

Employing the written rather than the spoken word, Milton in
his prose frequently includes autobiographical "digressions" as
a way of importing into his text the eloquence of example his
readers would otherwise be unable to discern. The strategy
reflects the introspective quality typical of Puritan writers, but
also indicative of his rigorous Protestantism is Milton's unwillingness to credit his own virtues or labors with the fulfillment of
his aspirations. Thus offsetting the potential for pride latent in
his concern for self-vindication is his persistent acknowledgment
that nothing in his own power can guarantee the muse's favor.
Puritan preachers for the most part cultivated learning not

because they saw it as essential to their ministry but as a means of practicing self-denial, of placing themselves wholly at God's disposal.[9] Similarly the poet must consecrate himself to God's service, denying his physical desires and striving to prepare himself through study. At the same time he must realize that just as his scholarship alone cannot produce verse that will live, so his chaste life cannot earn him the inspiration he seeks. The muse must come "unimplor'd" (IX.22), not at the poet's call but awaiting the time appointed by God to press him into service. Like Christ and the Lady, he must exert himself to the utmost in preparing himself for his vocation, but he must credit his success to the divine sanction that alone makes his work truly worthy. Remarking on Gideon's diligence in preparing for battle despite God's promise that he will conquer the Midianites, the Puritan divine Richard Rogers counsels all Christians to imitate the sort of behavior that Milton's narrator manifests: "And so we ought to use ordinary meanes to bring any worke to passe appointed us of God, though we have the promise of good successe from him, and yet againe on the other side, we should not attribute any thing to them, for that were to detract from God his due."[10]

Even without explicitly referring to himself, the poet impresses the stamp of his own character on his verse, as the divine quality of the Lady's song indicates. The Word that purifies the soul also illuminates speech. A transformation of this kind, however, is integral to the discourse of all Christians. The prophetic poet, like the true preacher, must receive an additional call, a heavenly warrant for action that permits his words to reflect not only his own purity but his special access to divine truth. Just as Christ in *Paradise Regained* receives an insight into God's design that issues in the words which conquer Satan, so the narrator of *Paradise Lost* must first be granted a vision of the Word as idea, *ratio*, before he can respond to the Word through utterance, *oratio*.

In their innocence Adam and Eve are able apparently at will to repay their Creator in words appropriate to his beneficence, but the bard's physical blindness is in part a sign of his first father's disobedience. Thus the Book of Nature, so clear to

Adam, presents the narrator "with a Universal blanc" (III.48) which can only be remedied through inward illumination. "This *World* is such a *Book* of *God*," Peter Sterry observes, "in which you have a *Representation* of him, but so confus'd; that it is impossible to know any thing of God aright by the *Natural Image*, except you have first the *Spiritual Image*, which is God himself form'd in your Souls."[11] Like Augustine in the *Confessions* and Adam after the Fall, the narrator is stimulated to pray, and his human words allow him to approach the inner Word that is both the impetus and the goal for his quest. But the effect of the vision he receives is at once to impart knowledge and to provide the words necessary to convey that knowledge to his readers. His inner eye must be cleared, he says, "that I may see and tell / Of things invisible to mortal sight" (III.54-55).

Although the artist looks to God for the success of his undertaking, his own powers are not negated but rather transformed by the inspiration he receives. Even the Old Testament prophets, commentators note, delivered their sacred messages in the idiom and voice they customarily employed, and George Wither counters the claims of antirationalist visionaries by insisting that a true prophet must "himselfe have also a true understanding of the Interpretations of that which is represented unto him."[12] Likewise Augustine distinguishes between imitation, in which a performer simply copies what God has produced, and true art. For Sidney the poet's sacred character lies in his being a maker whose act of creation is analogous to God's because he translates a "foreconceit" into a tangible reality. "Onely the Poet," he says, "lifted up with the vigor of his owne invention, dooth growe in effect another nature, in making things either better then Nature bringeth forth, or, quite a newe, formes such as never were in Nature . . . so as he goeth hand in hand with Nature, not inclosed within the narrow warrant of her guifts, but freely ranging onely within the Zodiack of his owne wit." While Sidney confesses that the poet's ideas are ultimately from God, his stress lies on the artist's freedom to create a second nature of his own devising, in some ways superior to the original.[13] Augustine, on the other hand, though he agrees that the artist's task is to express a preexisting concept, is much more emphatic in identifying the foreconceit of true art with the one that underlies God's creation. Aided by divine illumination, the artist apprehends the principles on which Nature is created, and thus he continues the process God has set in motion.[14]

To Augustine, then, artists neither copy God's creation nor supplant it with their own; rather, using their particular skills and their own idiom, they give expression to the intent they perceive with the help of an inward light. Although Nature cannot itself provide saving knowledge of God, once that knowledge is implanted through grace, God's purposes can be discerned in the natural order, the Word glossing the Book of Nature much as Raphael does for Adam. But if there was general agreement that the poet must respond in kind to the form of God's creation, nonetheless Protestants diverged widely in their perception of God's foreconceit, and consequently they disagreed on the character their response must assume. Bunyan for instance argues, in an inversion of classical standards, that the world is too serious, his divine subject too urgent, for him to employ a style as fully adorned as he is capable of: "I dare not: *God* did not play in convincing of me; the *Devil* did not play in tempting of me; neither did I play when I sunk as into a bottomless pit, when *the pangs of hell caught hold upon me*: wherefore I may not play in my relating of them, but be plain and simple."[15] Yet Donne employs a similar appeal to God's example in order to justify the elaborate style of his *Devotions*:

> But thou art also (*Lord* I intend it to thy *glory*, and let no *prophane mis-interpreter* abuse it to thy *diminution*) thou art a *figurative*, a *metaphoricall God* too: A *God* in whose words there is such a height of *figures*, such *voyages*, such *peregrinations* to fetch remote and precious *metaphors*, such *extensions*, such *spreadings*, such *Curtaines* of *Allegories*, such *third Heavens* of *Hyperboles*, so *harmonious eloquutions*, so *retired* and so *reserved* expressions, so *commanding perswasions*, so *perswading commandements*, such *sinewes* even in thy *milke*, and such *things* in thy *words*, as all *prophane Authors*, seeme of the seed of the *Serpent*, that *creepes*; thou art the *dove*, that flies.[16]

In *Paradise Lost* Milton gives us both versions of God. Bunyan's stern and sober deity appears primarily in Book III, speaking the precise theological language that caused Pope to characterize him as a "School-Divine." But Donne's oblique God, while presented less explicitly, is in fact more pervasive, his indirection revealed not so much in the words he speaks as in the effects he achieves through the Word. In *Paradise Regained* the Incarnate Word realizes his dual nature simultaneously with acquiring a language capable of expressing the miracle he represents. Through most of *Paradise Lost*, however, God's beneficence is articulated most fully in the Book of Nature, whose origins Raphael describes to Adam and Eve in Book VII. And just as the angel attributes the elaborate and various manifestation of God's bounty to a divine command, so the epic narrator reveals that the principles upon which the Creation unfolds have been first enunciated in the colloquy between the Father and the Son. Thus Milton reconciles Bunyan's God with Donne's, showing that the expansiveness and obliquity of the latter is based upon the solemnity and precision of the former. At the same time Milton's artistry like God's fulfills and gives material form to the divine intent that sets it in motion, all the while acknowledging and celebrating its source. For if God's creation returns to its Maker in gestures of praise and gratitude, the epic voice credits not just the heavenly Word but, through allusion, the Scriptural Word as providing the impetus, establishing the principles and setting the limits, for his own creation.

[II]

In the heavenly colloquy of Book III we have Milton's closest approximation to the stern God of Bunyan. The episode has sparked a critical debate over whether Milton should have presented God as a speaking character, or how he might have made him more appealing. The issue ultimately involves questions about one's view of deity that are not susceptible to critical resolution, but within the strictures of Augustine's concept of artistic creation,. the episode itself is essential, the style inevitable. Speaking in curt, precise language, the Father renders as nearly as possible the pure idea, the foreconceit of Creation and redemption. Thus the dialogue answers the prayer for knowledge with which the narrator begins the book, and the special illumination continues to sustain his flight through "Empyreal Air" (VII.14) at least until he returns in Book VII to his "Native Element" (VII.16). But if through the Father we perceive the divine intent underlying the Creation, through the dialogue between him and the Son we have revealed to us the pattern according to which idea is translated into action, *ratio* into *oratio*. As the Son acknowledges that the mercy he manifests is latent in the Father's appeal to justice, so the Creation, despite the complexity and particularity with which it is realized, discloses its continuing dependence upon the principles of order and goodness which underlie its variety.

Like the characterization of the Father, the exchange between him and the Son is the subject of controversy. Those who find the colloquy to be a genuine Socratic dialogue, in which the Son becomes aware of his role only gradually, accept at least implicitly Milton's theological Arianism or his "subordinationism." Others, finding the exchange to be ritualistic, argue for the orthodoxy of the passage.[17] Without more information from Milton on the subject, the theological dispute seems to me insoluble, but whether or not the colloquy is necessary for the Son, it is clearly essential for the angels and for Milton's readers.

Even to angels God in his essence is unknowable. In his anger "the sacred hill" (VI.25) is darkened, but at his most beatific he is only "a voice / From midst a Golden Cloud" (VI.27-28), the inhabitant of "a flaming Mount, whose top / Brightness had made invisible" (V.598-599). Unlike Satan, who wills his own obscurity, God progressively reveals himself through the agency of the Word. Primarily the Word operates through the Son, who physically reflects the goodness of divine will simultaneously with its declaration. As God forecasts the success of Satan's mission and promises to temper justice with mercy,

Beyond compare the Son of God was seen
Most glorious, in him all his Father shone
Substantially express'd, and in his face

Divine compassion visibly appear'd,
Love without end, and without measure Grace.

(III.138-142)

But the Word, as Henry Vane points out, is not simply the
second person of the Trinity but "the witness it self, which is
born by all the three." "[T]his living Word of God is that
whereby God speaks forth himself perfectly and distinctly, to the
understanding both of himself and of the creature."[18] Thus just
as God's terse prophecy becomes both accessible and beautiful
by being reflected in the Son, his words themselves are also a
means of revelation, and they have a sensory effect on the angels
who hear them: "while God spake, ambrosial fragrance fill'd /
All Heav'n, and in the blessed Spirits elect / Sense of new joy
ineffable diffus'd" (III.135-137). Endowed with their capacity to
unite spirit and sense, to feel ideas, the angels immediately
experience the goodness implicit in God's statement. Milton's
fallen readers, on the other hand, because they lack the ability to
perceive the beauty in abstract truth, cannot find the plan fully
satisfying without the more extended elaboration provided first
by the colloquy and finally by the Creation itself.

While the larger audience requires a relatively full explanation of God's intentions, the Son grasps the import of the
Father's plan almost immediately. His initial praise and rhetorical questions show he has intuited much of the Father's motives
without having heard them articulated, but he persists in the
exchange in order to manifest the divine plan, to make it accessible to lesser creatures. At the same time, despite the Son's
apparent softening of the Father's position, they both make clear
that the details of the plan are not an *ad hoc* reaction to Satan's
maneuvering but are implicit in the original idea. To the Son's
perception that withholding grace would be to allow Satan his
triumph, the Father replies, "All hast thou spok'n as my
thoughts are, all / As my Eternal purpose hath decreed"
(III.171-172), and he concludes with a declaration that invites a
further response: "He with his whole posterity must die, / Die
hee or Justice must; unless for him / Some other able, and as

willing, pay / The rigid satisfaction, death for death" (III.209-212). Like Satan in the demonic council, the Father at least knows the result of the dialogue beforehand, but here there is no manipulation to determine the outcome. While Satan adjourns the proceedings before his followers can diminish his glory with an empty gesture, the pause before the Son's volunteering and the absence of any attempt to forestall other candidates indicate that there is no effort to grant the Son anything the others are unwilling to concede. And so whether the Son is aware of the plan from the first or whether he grows to realize the meaning of his Sonship only as its significance unfolds for the onlookers, the colloquy serves at once to establish the pattern for the manifestation of God's intentions and to distinguish his foreknowledge, which does not preclude choice, from the predetermined results of the conclave.

In the same way that the Son makes progressively more clear the implications latent in the divine idea, the language of the Father itself discloses with increasing fullness the reality which the words bring into being. At least in part, the complaints about the Father's style are the result of a failure to distinguish between divine and human speech. For while they share an expressive function, the relationship of sign to referent is fundamentally different in the two verbal systems. Human words are subsequent to and dependent upon the things they signify; the words of God on the other hand bear the same relationship to their referents as spirit to matter in Milton's theology. They are not only signs but the ontological basis for their referents, both prior to and inclusive of the reality they indicate. The result is a congruence between God's words and their referents even more perfect than Adam's unfallen discourse enjoys. The Father's word "Grace," for instance, is itself "gracious" (III.142, 144), and in a comparable passage Raphael quotes God, who declares his intention to create in recompense for Satan's rebellion

> Another World, out of one man a Race
> Of men innumerable, there to dwell,
> Not here, till by degrees of merit rais'd
> They open to themselves at length the way

Up hither, under long obedience tri'd,
And Earth be chang'd to Heav'n, and Heav'n to Earth,
One Kingdom, Joy and Union without end.

(VII.155-161)

The chiasmus in line 160 recalls a similar reversal in Satan's speech: "The mind is its own place, and in itself / Can make a Heav'n of Hell, a Hell of Heav'n" (I.254-255). Yet despite his bravado, Satan comes to acknowledge his inability to change reality. In God's speech, however, the syntactical reversal reflects divine intention, and thus the utterance is the virtual accomplishment, its manifestation in human time an inevitable result of God's having spoken.

A similar passage occurs in the colloquy, where the Father explains his course of action toward the pair whose fall he foreknows. He decrees,

Man therefore shall find grace,
The other none: in Mercy and Justice both,
Through Heav'n and Earth, so shall my glory excel,
But Mercy first and last shall brightest shine.

(III.131-134)

The exchange that follows demonstrates the meaning of "Mercy first and last." The Son will enable Adam and Eve to repent, and then provide them with an internal paradise in mitigation of their banishment from Eden. But the sentence itself, with the Word "Mercy" both preceding and following the word "Justice," already accomplishes what the colloquy makes explicit and what the events subsequent to the Fall translate into history. And as God's words anticipate the behavior of the things to which they refer, so even the tone bears a decorous resemblance to the subject. The austerity and judicial precision of the Father's language is a part of the expression of the Law, which implies but does not manifest the Gospel's doctrine of love. It remains, appropriately, for the Son, in his compassionate offer to sacrifice himself, to provide the tonal relief as well as the doctrinal tempering of justice with mercy.

When God's decrees refer to eternal matters, his speech has a high incidence of abstract nouns that are likewise immutable in meaning and use. But when God speaks of temporal subjects, his language must take into account the fact that creation is mutable, that its realization of the divine idea is progressive rather than immediate. While God never puns or obscures meaning as Satan does, his language is capable not only of expressing his eternal declarations but also of elucidating and thus controlling the divided and confusing postlapsarian world. The permutations God practices on the word "will" in the following passage are a case in point:

> Man shall not quite be lost, but sav'd who will,
> Yet not of will in him, but grace in me
> Freely voutsaf't; once more I will renew
> His lapsed powers, though forfeit and enthrall'd
> By sin to foul exorbitant desires.   (III.173-177)

An aspect of centripetal, Satanic repetition is the consistency with which the speaker employs the word as the same part of speech, providing an illusion of stability as a facade behind which to work his radical subversions of meaning. God, however, varies form and usage as the sentence develops, indicating the changes in meaning it is the purpose of the statement to clarify. Altering "will" from verb to noun and changing its referent from human to divine, God reveals both the malleability of the human will and its dependence upon the will of God. The first usage is latently ambiguous. Is it active, meaning "to will" and implying human sufficiency, or passive, meaning "to be willing" and thus positing an external agent? The subsequent usages resolve the dilemma by replacing the original pronominal antecedent "Man" with the divine first person singular. Man's fallen will, transformed from verb to noun, is shown to be static and impotent, while God's will, active and efficacious, becomes the agent for restoring to man the passive receptiveness of which even fallen will is capable. Thus all the meanings finally obtain, with the repetitions sorting out the appropriate referents.

Although God's plan becomes more fully elaborated, its good-

ness more apparent, as the dialogue progresses, even the compassion of the Son is expressed in language that is abstract,
precise, theological. As the Christ of *Paradise Regained* acknowledges, however, he must devise a medium sufficiently complex to
communicate the transcendent nature of his message, to suggest
the miracle he represents. In neither epic do we see the Incarnate Word employing the language of parable and metaphor
with which the temptations equip him, but in *Paradise Lost* we
find Donne's extravagant, oblique God manifested in the activi-
ties of the creating Word. In the same way that the Father's first
decree establishes the principle whose implications the colloquy
elucidates, so Creation is initiated by a command and preceded
by the Son's activity as a geometer:

> . . . in his hand
> He took the golden Compasses, prepar'd
> In God's Eternal store, to circumscribe
> This Universe, and all created things:
> One foot he centred, and the other turn'd
> Round through the vast profundity obscure,
> And said, Thus far extend, thus far thy bounds,
> This be thy just Circumference, O World.   (VI.224-231)

But the idea will never be fully realized. In Milton's epic Nature
is presented not as a finished product but as an ongoing process,
various and complex. Similarly for Luther the Creation is a
continuing miracle, and the Son is the agent of God's constant
reaffirmation:

> And it is Christ the Lord, who was present at the time of the
> creation of all things not as a mere spectator but as a coequal
> Creator and Worker, who still governs and preserves all and
> will continue to govern and preserve all until the end of the
> world. . . . In the doctrine of creation it is of primary impor-
> tance that we know and believe that God has not withdrawn
> His sustaining hand from His handiwork.[19]

That Creation is the ongoing articulation of the Word is
revealed in its structure, which replicates in concrete form the

complex pattern of unfolding and return that defines the colloquy between Father and Son in Book III. As God's love is
extended, made accessible by being expressed in words, so the
angels respond to divine beneficence "With Jubilee, and loud
Hosannas" (III.348). At the same time they recapitulate with
physical gestures the ceremonious quality which the use of
apostrophe has lent to the divine dialogue: "Towards either
Throne they bow, and to the ground / With solemn adoration
down they cast / Thir Crowns inwove with Amarant and Gold"
(III.350-352). Similarly Creation responds to its source in gestures of praise and thanksgiving, and it continues the enlarge-
ment of God's love by obeying his command to procreate. If
Raphael in describing the first days of Creation employs metaphors of sexual intercourse and generation as a way to accommodate the events to Adam's experience, the metaphor becomes
literal as the Creation becomes more particularized. From the
Spirit's "brooding wings" (VII.235), Raphael moves to "The
Earth . . . in the Womb as yet / Of Waters, Embryon immature"
(VII.276-277), and at last he repeats the divine injunction, "Be
fruitful, multiply" (VII.396). But despite the increasing detail,
the force that animates Nature continues to be apparent.[20]

Adam and Eve are the latest of God's creations and thus the
most particularized and independent. But their happiness, as
they acknowledge in their hymns, depends like the rest of Creation upon the order God establishes, and their relationship,
satisfying in itself yet capable of infinite growth, adheres to the
pattern set by the Father and Son for the perpetual unfolding of
divine beneficence. For fallen humanity, to whom mutability
suggests only the limits of their own lives, this sense of incompleteness can be frustrating, but in the prelapsarian Garden the
experience of God's love in ongoing Creation has the effect of
continuously sustaining and renewing human sensibility. Because Creation always exists in potential as well as actuality,
change brings a perpetual exfoliation which in itself contains no
necessary withering. "Universal *Pan*," we are told, "Knit with
the *Graces* and the *Hours* in dance / Led on th'Eternal Spring"
(IV.266-268).

Through Raphael's description, or by approximating God's

vision, we can recognize that the act of Creation is simply one stage in the continuing revelation of divine love, and that its development occurs in the orderly fashion dictated by its governing principles. From the perspective of unfallen humanity, however, the Book of Nature manifests its author often in oblique ways. As Adam's dialogue with Raphael in Book VIII shows, the circuitous route to discovery is frequently the most effective, and a part of the delight of Eden lies in its consistently offering the unexpected, leading to destinations by indirect means that serve further to acquaint the human couple with the rich variety and complexity of God's love as the Garden manifests it. To be sure, we cannot read about the Garden's "wanton growth" (IV.629), the "mazy error" (IV.239) of the flowing brooks, even the elephant's wreathing "His Lithe Proboscis" (IV.347), without anticipating the serpent's "Gordian twine" (IV.348) and the Satanic deviousness that it figures. Yet while in Satan's service the intricately weaving form of the serpent indicates his attempt to obscure his own designs, still in Eden its shape remains simply another instance of the ongoing richness and beauty of Nature which protects innocence from boredom.

[III]

Although its path is at times circuitous, Creation properly glossed works always to reveal the Word which speaks it into being, to enlarge the goodness latent in the divine idea. In their hymns Adam and Eve return to the Word the words of praise and gratitude God's beneficence inspires, and the narrator and his opponent Satan likewise respond in their own ways to the principles of Creation they discern. Seeking to rival God, Satan rejects the grounding of divine artisty in truth and instead appropriates its obliquity to serve the purpose of deception. But despite his attempts to glorify himself through his work, his products inevitably reflect the perversity of the mind that conceives them. Milton's narrator on the other hand, freely acknowledging his debt to the inner oracle and to Scriptures, responds by continuing in human words the variety and complexity of the divine Creation. And while Satan's imitation of God's creative act seeks to obscure its source and goals, the indirection of the narrator's verse serves to involve the reader in a process which offers like its original a progressive revelation of God's ways.

Satan is a debased version of the Sidneyan poet, copying God by creating from his own mind. But to mimic God's creative act is to parody divine art. For while God's creation is ongoing, opening outward in a continuing disclosure of his beneficence, the form of Satanic artifice mirrors the mind of its author. It is enclosed and self-regarding, attempting to insulate itself from any measure external to its own boundaries. Like the partial song and sweet discourse with which the fallen angels divert themselves after Satan's departure, Pandemonium is in itself splendid, its Baroque visual effects matched by "the sound / Of Dulcet Symphonies and voices sweet" (I.711-712) that accompanies its rise. Yet Mammon's triumph is illusory because it does not originate in a positive response to the divine love that enriches its heavenly prototype. Instead the manner of its creation is described in metaphors which suggest the violence and perversity of its architects. Mammon's crew, we are told, "Op'n'd into the Hill a spacious wound / And digg'd out ribs of Gold" (I.689-690), and following his example people will rifle "the bowels of thir mother Earth" (I.687). The finished product, moreover, is employed in ways which reflect the corruption of its origins. Its absence of genuine glory seems obliquely to be expressed in the sham debate it houses, and despite the symphonies accompanying the completion of the building, the council manifests its amity by erupting in discordant noise. As at the dissolution of the Stygian council, the devils voice their approval of Mammon's advice in a way appropriate to its lack of substance:

> . . . such murmur fill'd
> Th'Assembly, as when hollow Rocks retain
> The sound of blust'ring winds, which all night long
> Had rous'd the Sea, now with hoarse cadence lull
> Sea-faring men o'erwatcht, whose Bark by chance

Or Pinnace anchors in a craggy Bay
After the Tempest . . . (II.284-290)

The hollowness with which the din reverberates suggests how thinly Hell is partitioned from Chaos, but the encouragement the devils receive from their echo indicates how successful Satanic creation is at involving its auditors in a world of its own defining.

The image of the Satanic mind that is impressed on his architecture is even more apparent in his accidental offspring Sin and Death. The allegorical mode itself can be regarded as Satanic because of its dualism, its separation of abstract and concrete; and together with Satan his children are clearly intended as a parody of the Trinity.[21] But the relationship among the three enacts as well the movement of the sinful mind as Augustine and Luther describe it. While in *Paradise Lost* the figure of human marriage is the fullest concrete realization of divine love, to Augustine fornication is a metaphor for the soul's pursuit of pleasure apart from God: "So the soul commits fornication when she turns away from you and tries to find outside you things which, unless she returns to you, cannot be found in their true and pure state."[22] Luther draws upon Augustine's terminology in distinguishing between grace and nature:

> But grace is never content in the things which it sees except as it sees God in and above them, and it wills, hopes, and rejoices in the fact that all things exist, are seen, and are accomplished for the glory of God. Nature, on the contrary, thinks that all the things it sees are nothing unless they serve to its advantage, exist for it and are done for it. And then it esteems them, if it can appropriate them for its own benefit, use, and good.
>
> This is spiritual fornication, iniquity, and a terrible curving in on itself.[23]

Like Luther's fallen nature, Satan seeks his own advantage and as a result begets Sin in his own image. Their fornication in turn produces Death, whose constant reenactment of his father's incest results in the offspring that return, gnawing, to their mother's womb. The escalating gruesomeness of the account yields a progressive revelation of the evil mind. Self-regarding, it creates in its own image, but its lust becomes increasingly self-destructive because, cut off from the sustenance of divine love, the product returns to its author only his own consuming energy.

The solipsistic form of Satan's creations is the result of his serving as his own muse. Milton's narrator, however, hopes to transcend the limits of his own imagination through divine assistance. The epic voice seems deliberately to equivocate about the precise identity of his muse, but in the present context the Spirit's significance lies in its being the instrument also of God's creation: "Thou from the first / Wast present, and with mighty wings outspread / Dove-like satst brooding on the vast Abyss / And mad'st it pregnant" (I.19-22). By specifying this particular heavenly power, the narrator seeks not so much to supersede God's artistry as to acquire the knowledge necessary to augment divine revelation in a way that is faithful to the principles which govern the original. Thus in Book VII Milton through Raphael describes the origins of the material universe, showing how in its progressive unfolding it continues to manifest the divine idea that is its source. Likewise the narrator seeks to disclose the intention he perceives in the heavenly colloquy, and in the same way that the Creation persists in acknowledging and celebrating the Word, the epic voice repeatedly confesses his reliance upon the inward illumination that reveals to him the terms on which he may "justify the ways of God to men" (I.26).

But while Adam has Raphael to help him interpret the Book of Nature, after the Fall the Scriptural Word is humanity's primary source of revelation. And just as artists are not limited to copying Nature, so on biblical subjects they are not confined to the actual words of Scripture. In his preface to the *Poems*, Abraham Cowley argues that sacred poets must do more than simply turn "a story of the *Scripture*, like *Mr. Quarles's*, or some other godly matter, like Mr. *Heywood of Angels*, into *Rhyme*."[24] Similarly Milton observes, "It is not hard for any man, who hath a Bible in his hands, to borrow good words and holy sayings in abundance; but to make them his own, is a work of grace onely from above" (*Eikon*; CPW, 3: 553). Milton echoes the Scriptures often in *Paradise Lost*, most frequently in Book VII, and if he extends and elaborates upon what he finds there, still he recognizes his debt and preserves what is explicitly set forth. Continuing the revelation of divine purpose he perceives through inward vision, he persistently reminds us not only of the ultimate but of the intermediate source of his song, the Scriptural Word which provides the order and sets the limits on his own creation.

Despite his recurrently attributing his poem to a divine source, Milton's narrator does not speak an Edenic language. Even Thomas Sprat admitted that the defenders of virtue must acquire the tainted skills of eloquence in order to combat their exploitation by evil people, and in *Paradise Lost* it is clear that the way to defeat Satanic duplicity is not to retreat from the possibilities of language but to recover them for their proper use.[25] While in the war Satan has developed for deceptive purposes the physical potential latent in his spiritual substance, the divine response is not to destroy the physical but to reclaim it through the creation of a material universe. Similarly, although Satan introduces ambiguity into language, God reverses its implications, turning meaninglessness to rewarding variety and consequently making the corruption of words a *felix culpa*. Thus as the manifestation of God's goodness in Nature is more complete because its route is circuitous, so Milton's verse can communicate the difficulty of its subject only by being likewise complex and indirect, playing etymology against contemporary meaning, distorting syntax, alluding to events apparently remote from what he is describing. Yet the difference between demonic and redeemed speech does not lie exclusively in its use, as Sprat's concession to eloquence seems to imply. Rather, through divine inspiration the style itself is transformed, becoming an instrument capable not simply of persuading or manipulating its auditors but of illuminating them, of engaging them in the same process of revelation begun in the Creation and continued in Scriptures.

Like the style that the Word adopts for both God's books, Milton's poetry exerts a pressure always forward and outward, though not at the cost of rejecting or forgetting what has gone before. But while the narrator seeks to extend his reader's capacity to recall and perceive, Satan's rhetoric aims at disconti- nuity. Just as his protean personality can accommodate any number of roles without attempting to reconcile their inconsis- tencies, so his speech attempts to detach the present moment from past or future and thus to insulate words from any external referent, making them subject to whatever meanings he chooses to impose. Satan strives, that is, to achieve the same Lethean effect that Comus attributes to Circe and the Sirens: "they in pleasing slumber lull'd the sense, / And in sweet madness robb'd it of itself" (260-261). The narrator, on the other hand, emulates the Lady, whose singing causes Comus to feel "a sacred and home-felt delight, / . . . sober certainty of waking bliss" (262-263). The difference between the two effects is the same one that the Cambridge Platonist John Smith employs to distinguish true prophecy from false:

> Now from what hath been said ariseth one main Characteris- tical distinction between the *Prophetical* and *Pseudo-prophetical* spirit, viz. That the *Prophetical* spirit doth never alienate the Mind, (seeing it seats it self as well in the *Rational* powers as in the *Sensitive*,) but alwaies maintains a consistency and clearness of Reason, strength and soliditie of Judgment, where it comes; it doth not *ravish* the Mind, but *inform* and *enlighten* it: But the *Pseudo-prophetical* spirit, if indeed without any kind of dissimulation it enters into any one, because it can rise no higher then the Middle region of Man, which is his *Phansy*, it there dwells as in storms and tempests.[26]

Adam learns, we have discovered, by becoming engaged in a dialectic between external and internal revelation, the new data he encounters evoking and elaborating upon what he already knows. But where Adam is led to perceive the Word in the complex and ongoing process of the physical Creation, the fallen reader must replicate Adam's experience of progressive revela- tion through the words of the true prophet-poet.

Stanley Fish has argued that Milton entangles us recurrently in his rhetoric in order to chasten us, to make us aware of the limitations of our reason and of the extent to which we are of the devil's party.[27] The pattern Fish describes may always exist for some readers, and certainly it is experienced at some points by most of us. Yet it seems to me that the poet in general attempts self-consciously to avoid exercising through his words the demonic control over his auditors that Fish's analysis implies. Instead of experiencing the poem as a series of set pieces in which the reader perpetually reenacts the drama of fall and redemption, or at least existing in tension with that experience, is the sense of the narrative as a steady and gradual elaboration of its theme. In response to T. S. Eliot's complaints, twentieth-century critics have labored to catalogue the subtleties of Milton's verse, and the devices and effects they have discovered defy even citation, much less summary. A few, however, are especially important to the effect of progressive unfolding I am attempting to define. In the first place, the blank verse itself, its "sense variously drawn out" from one line to the next, is a principal means of achieving this sense of progression, and the syntax is another. C. S. Lewis has remarked, "Milton avoids discontinuity by an avoidance of what grammarians call the simple sentence," and the first period of the poem, its meaning building line by line, clause by clause, is a good illustration of the effect Milton and Lewis are describing.[28] But if we are constantly drawn onward, we are like Adam led also through the constant appeal to memory to accept each new phenomenon as a clarification of what we have previously encountered, to find in every experience the manifestation of a potential latent in the original idea.

Milton accomplishes this effect largely by repeating events and crucial terms throughout the poem. The Creation, for instance, is mentioned or described at least three times before Book VII; and within the first hundred lines of Book I, Milton has established the moral vocabulary and system of symbols against which subsequent episodes are explicitly measured. In his study of Miltonic repetition Leslie Brisman notes the tension between the poem's iterations and the sense of time as unorganized flux which the reader brings to the poem: "The return of the verse contrasts with and acknowledges the irrevocable disparity from human experience in time, from the hard fact that there is no return."[29] For Brisman the most important effect is to allow a momentary arrest of time's progress, but while the reader requires the fixed points of reference that both God and the narrator provide, the stasis of the simple return is the property only of Satanic repetition. Despite Satan's iconoclasm and the discontinuities among the various positions he takes, he has a vital interest in resisting the unfolding of time, for God's progressive revelation entails Satan's corresponding diminution. Thus his seditious acts have an underlying motive of retrogression, of returning to a *status quo* he deems more acceptable.

He initially rebels because he feels the Son's begetting has been at the expense of his former privileged position, and one of his hopes in tempting Adam and Eve is that he can force God to recall the Creation. This aspect of Satan's character is dominant in *Paradise Regained*, where he perceives more fully that mutability, the medium of experience his success with Adam and Eve introduces into the world, will be the vehicle for his undoing. Consequently in tempting Christ he hopes to delay the end of his "Reign on Earth so long enjoy'd" (I.125), and he adopts a repetitious strategy which reveals, in its futile attempt to arrest time, his fear of the future. In a series of similes which progressively depersonalize Satan, reducing him to an elemental force whose motion is purely causal, Milton describes him as incapable of adjusting his approach to meet altered circumstances:

> But as a man who had been matchless held
> In cunning, overreach't where least he thought,
> To salve his credit, and for very spite
> Still will be tempting him who foils him still,
> And never cease, though to his shame the more;
> Or as a swarm of flies in vintage time,
> About the wine-press where sweet must is pour'd,
> Beat off, returns as oft with humming sound;
> Or surging waves against a solid rock,
> Though all to shivers dash't, th'assault renew,
> Vain batt'ry, and in froth or bubbles end;
> So Satan, whom repulse upon repulse
> Met ever, and to shameful silence brought,
> Yet gives not o'er though desperate of success,
> And his vain importunity pursues.   (IV.10-24)

Barbara Lewalski has said of Satan's notion of time in the brief epic, "This conception of historical pattern as eternal recurrence and this compulsive attitude toward time lead Satan to base his temptations of Christ upon the premise that Christ's behaviour must inevitably repeat the patterns set by men before him." The Son, on the other hand, grows to appreciate a concept of history that is eschatological, seeing that, as Lewalski puts it, "what *has been* is the appropriate starting point but not the fixed definition of what *will be*. The historical process is seen to be linear, not cyclical, and Christian typology is shown to involve progress, redefinition, and re-creation."[30] The contrasting views of time are reflected as well in the respective styles in *Paradise Lost*. Returning upon itself, Satanic repetition creates an illusion of familiarity which obscures the erosion of meaning he seeks to achieve. Redeemed human speech, however, like divine iteration in the heavenly colloquy, works to awaken judgment, to extend understanding. For if, as we encounter the same word again, we acknowledge the similarity with what has gone before, we also, by noting the change in form or application, measure the accretion of meaning, the resonances the word has acquired in the interim. And thus, recognizing we are involved in a process not yet completed, we are directed to look forward as well as back, to anticipate the further illumination that the future promises.

Style and structure, then, collaborate to move the reader forward within the poem in a process that builds upon or refines what we have already encountered, but the epic itself is not self-contained. Milton violates the boundaries of his story first of all by calling attention to the character of his persona and second by his reliance upon a heavenly muse for the execution of his calling. More important, however, is the consistent effort to relate the truth unfolding in his poem with the continuing revelation of God's purpose in the world to which the reader belongs. By such devices as simile, allusion, prolepsis, and typological symbolism, Milton brings to bear on each episode a complex of reinforcing and elaborating contexts, not only within the poem but external to it. Thus the epic itself opens out, asking us to measure the resonances of Satan's revolt and the human fall throughout the subsequent history of Adam's descendants, a history which is still ongoing but whose conclusion the poem foretells.

Grace subsequent to the Fall is first manifested in Adam as the restoration of memory, for he begins to overcome despair only when he remembers the prophecy in which the hope of humankind resides. But as Adam cannot forget his sin even when he is redeemed from it, neither are Milton's readers asked to recover Paradise on the same terms our first parents held it. In his effort to acquaint us with the internal Eden "happier far" (XII.587), the narrator must first of all receive a vision of divine purpose and second acquire the means appropriate to convey his knowledge. But as he discovers, the medium is implicit in the idea, the form of his *oratio* provided by the *ratio* that underlies the manifestation of the Word in Creation and history. Thus although like Satan he exploits the sinuosity and ambiguity latent in words, through divine inspiration the epic voice is able to reform these characteristics, to employ them to the end of heightened awareness rather than of the deception they serve under Satan's influence. Where Satan's rhetoric is tyrannical, imposing meanings on words and seeking to force the wills of his listeners, the narrator like God employs a liberating style, both clarifying the options available and permitting the auditor freely to choose his course. Yet because Satan has rendered the relationship between human words and their referents problematic, the language that stands against his cannot emulate the precision and directness of God's words in Book III. In order to communicate to fallen minds the goodness implicit in God's edicts, the narrator must approximate in his poetry the same complexity through which God, with Raphael's aid, reveals himself to Adam and Eve in the Book of Nature. Just as the Creation indirectly recoups the damage of Satan's rebellion, taking his corrupt use of matter as an occasion to extend divine beneficence, so the fall of language must also be made fortunate, and the agency for redeeming words is the Word which redeems humanity. Through the intercession of the heavenly muse, Satanic duplicity is converted to the fruitful obliquity that enables God to reveal himself with ever increasing fullness.

CHAPTER SIX

Samson Agonistes and the "Trivial Weapon" of Words

T HE fall of Adam's speech and its recovery is a subject that is central to all the temptation poems. The Lady in *Comus* and the Christ of *Paradise Regained* reveal the spiritual condition upon which redeemed speech is predicated, and the narrator of *Paradise Lost* demonstrates its practice. But it is in *Samson Agonistes* that we find the complete pattern, the spiritual renewal together with the verbal redemption, most fully articulated.[1] Like many of Milton's contemporaries, Samson has come to distrust language, to seek to insulate himself from the capacity of words for ambiguity and deception. But like Christ in *Paradise Regained* or the narrator of *Paradise Lost*, Samson responds to the call to service only subsequent to mastering a means of expression appropriate to his faith. Ultimately he acquires this language inexplicably, through the inspiration of the internal Word, but as Adam has discovered in the last books of the epic that the fallen mind arrives at truth through the encounter with its opposite, so Samson in some measure prepares for his insight by exploring the limits and the possibilities of the kinds of language he and his visitors employ.

Although Samson has never enjoyed the capacity for Edenic speech, his effort to abjure verbal play is nonetheless a reversal of his previous attitude, for prior to his humiliation the biblical Samson is a bully who plays crude practical jokes and takes an unmerited pride in his verbal dexterity. As with the riddle his wedding guests solve, however, his reliance upon his wit and tongue to forestall Dalila's curiosity leads to disaster. Milton's Samson suffers the consequences of his Scriptural heritage. Appropriate to a figure whose pride has issued as often in words as in deeds, he falls the victim of his own "Shameful garrulity" (491), and his punishment for disclosing a holy secret, he thinks, is the revocation of the divine promise to employ him in an heroic enterprise. With the veracity and constancy of God's eternal decree thus called into question, human language becomes an even more uncertain medium. Subject now to the "daily fraud, contempt, abuse and wrong" (76) of his accustomed visitors, Samson becomes distrustful of words, fearful of their power and reluctant to credit their apparent meanings. Though he had once exploited the capacity of language for ambiguity and figurative meaning, he now views its polysemous quality with suspicion, requiring the Chorus to speak with a precision that admits no misconstructions. When they announce Harapha's approach by the self-consciously clever metaphor of an imminent storm, Samson responds, "Be less abstruse, my riddling days are past" (1064).

Through most of the poem, Samson behaves like a pietistic opponent of rhetoric, identifying words with the mutable and alien external world from which he must protect himself. Accepting this distrust as Milton's own position, Anne Ferry finds that "The poem itself . . . paradoxically denies the power of eloquence, of literature."[2] But even if we grant the possibility of a poem so absolutely self-consuming, it is difficult to read *Samson Agonistes* as an instance: we measure the protagonist's recovery in part by his growing control over language and reason, and he acquires the opportunity to fulfill God's promise not by renouncing words but by recovering his ability to exploit verbal ambiguity. Where before he had employed riddles as a means of flaunting his superiority over his enemies, by the end of his ordeal he adopts a metaphoric, ironic language that expresses both self-deprecation and faith in God. Resuming thus on new terms his role as riddle-master, Samson certifies his access to a spiritual understanding previously unavailable to him and at the same time provides himself the means to act upon his insight.

While Samson until his exchange with Harapha continues to distrust language, by the end of the poem he affirms its power as an instrument whose strength, like his own, derives from its apparent weakness.

[I]

If Samson manifests his heroism at the end of the poem through his regained control of figurative language, his self-torture at the outset lies in a literalism expressed in his masochistic obsession with paradox. Metaphor unites terms potentially disparate by viewing them from a perspective which discloses significant points of similarity; paradox, on the other hand, insists upon the discreteness of the terms by maintaining the ordinary, reasonable human viewpoint from which their irreconcilability is most noticeable. Limited through most of the poem to a concept of heroism derived from his earlier experience, Samson feels keenly the painful discrepancy between his previous role as God's champion and his present humiliation, between the promise he had been reared to fulfill and the frustrating conviction that his goal will be achieved without his participation. The reversal of his expectations forces him to recognize weaknesses his former glory had left undetected. "O impotence of mind, in body strong" (52), he laments in acknowledgment that his confidence of success was founded upon a virtue less self-sufficient than it seemed. The paradoxical vulnerability of his strength is matched by the irony of his seeking the sun in his blindness. "[D]ark in light" (75), he can find neither comfort in the "various objects of delight" (71) available in the visible world nor the means to resist his detractors, so that he feels himself "Inferior to the vilest now become / Of man or worm; the vilest here excel me, / They creep, yet see" (73-75). The refusal of contradictory facts to disclose a coherence, to yield to rational inquiry the means of their reconciliation, both tortures Samson and compels his attention, and so despite his aversion the language of paradox inhabits his speech and betrays his divided mind. Though in closing his lament he

reaches for a metaphor, equating his present condition with
burial, he rejects the figure because the differences between
death and his imprisonment override the similarities and make a
real grave preferable:

> As in the land of darkness yet in light,
> To live a life half dead, a living death,
> And buried; but O yet more miserable!
> Myself my Sepulcher, a moving Grave,
> Buried, yet not exempt
> By privilege of death and burial
> From worst of other evils, pains and wrongs,
> But made hereby obnoxious more
> To all the miseries of life,
> Life in captivity
> Among inhuman foes. (99-109)

The oppositions which define his life seem to collide with cruelly
destructive force because Samson thinks of them as existing in
the same plane: the physical, external, visible arena where his
previous victories were won.

Finding it impossible, from the perspective of his own self-
pity, to reconcile his chosenness with his present condition,
Samson concentrates his obsession with paradox on instruments
apparently inadequate to perform the tasks assigned them. His
initial way of dealing with the inappropriateness of his hair and
his eyes to their functions is to deny the significance of the ends
they fail to serve, discovering thus in their mutual meanness a
literal congruence between instrument and purpose. If his
strength is impotent "without a double share / Of wisdom"
(53-54), Samson sees its triviality underscored in the means of its
preservation: "God, when he gave me strength, to show withal /
How slight the gift was, hung it in my Hair" (58-59). While he
provisionally resolves the puzzle of his hair by denigrating what
it was to protect, he finds in the loss of his eyesight a paradox less
easily dismissed, but he later reconciles himself to the problem in
a similar way. In his opening monologue he questions without
apparent satisfaction the disparity between the importance of

sight and the vulnerability of the instrument to which it is entrusted:

> Since light so necessary is to life,
> And almost life itself, if it be true
> That light is in the Soul,
> She all in every part; why was the sight
> To such a tender ball as th'eye confin'd?
> So obvious and so easy to be quench't . . . (90-95)

But in his exchange with the Chorus he begins to value his physical sight less, discovering in his affliction a blessing which saves him from apprehending the full impact of his failure (195-199).

The bitter lesson Samson draws from the inadequacy of his hair as a guardian of his strength, the painful irony he feels in the vulnerability of his eyes despite their crucial function, are not the only inferences capable of being drawn from the objects whose meanness apparently disqualifies them for their assigned tasks. Samuel Johnson pronounced the frequent "allusions to low and trivial objects . . . unsuitable" for tragedy, but the very discrepancy that both Johnson and Samson find troubling is intrinsic to the biblical story and an aid to defining the terms on which the resolution of Milton's poem occurs, the nature of the middle Johnson failed to locate.[3] Both the Chorus and Samson refer to the jawbone with which he vanquished the "choicest youth" (264) of their captors as a "trivial weapon" (142; 263), and if neither is yet aware of the significance resident in the instrument's meanness, the commentators are plain. In his sermon on Psalms 102:16-17, the Smectymnuan Stephen Marshall alludes to the episode to illustrate God's power: "Sow a bad piece of ground, God doth not use to give a strong crop there; but it's quite otherwise in the building of the church, whatsoever the tooles or instruments are, it skills not one whit: Great instruments doe not further it, weak instruments cannot retard it: If he will fight, it's indifferent whether his weapon be a sword, or the jaw-bone of an Asse."[4] For Richard Rogers the motif is a recurrent one in the Book of Judges. About Gideon's dream,

whose results the Chorus describes in remarking on the fickleness of the Israelites (277-281), Rogers observes, "God doth his
people good by things which are of no reckoning nor account."
Even in the choice of the Danite Samson to be his deliverer,
Rogers finds God demonstrating a power so supreme he can
afford to be arbitrary: "[T]his tribe being one of the meanest: It
teacheth that God will serve himselfe by the meaner sort as well
as by the mightier and greater, when it pleaseth him."[5] Before
Samson can come to a similar understanding, however, he must
learn to define his heroism in a new way.

Like Oedipus, Samson is the riddle-master who has become
himself his own riddle, and while his stature as a tragic hero
depends upon his solving the enigma, his illumination is inseparable from the verbal process through which it is gained and
from his command of the ambiguous, metaphoric language in
which it is expressed. For Samson as for Milton's other protagonists, seeing and saying are mental operations inextricably
related; words are not simply a function of thought but the
means of thinking. Thus his spiritual recovery depends upon his
renewed ability to interpret metaphorically circumstances he has
previously regarded as paradoxical, and he regains this verbal
capacity in two steps. First, through the words of his visitors he
achieves an ironic detachment from his present condition that
allows him not simply to denigrate his eyes and his strength but
to appreciate the inner vision and virility for which his physical
sight and power are merely crude analogues, shadowy types.
And once he discerns the spiritual meaning latent in his physical
circumstances, he is able to resume his identity as a riddle-
master, acquiring the opportunity to vanquish his foes through
the renewed mastery of metaphor.

[II]

To the process of detachment Samson's visitors perform a
crucial if unintended function. Suspicious of words at the beginning of the poem, Samson only delays his restoration, for despair
is overcome by discovering a vocabulary whereby its causes and

nature can be expressed. Once objectified, whether through language or some other set of symbols, the despair seems less integral to the self and therefore capable of being transcended. As Adam has shown in Book X of *Paradise Lost*, even an unintelligible sigh can initiate the process of recovery that is sustained by the Word and that leads to a fuller command of redeemed speech. Samson's visitors, then, both provide him the opportunity to articulate his pain and are themselves, as many critics have demonstrated, symbols of the flaws Samson must excise before his regeneration can be complete. Rejecting their offers, he purges himself of the tendencies they represent.[6]

Milton's prefatory analogy to homeopathic medicine justifies the concepts of purgation, lustration, or catharsis in terms of which we ordinarily discuss the role of the visitors, and despite some disagreement over Milton's likely understanding of the terminology, its usefulness is borne out by the changes Samson undergoes.[7] But the effect of his visitors on Samson is more complex and variable than the analogy suggests, and by restricting ourselves to its terms we have been led to define their function too narrowly. Their importance, it seems to me, lies not just in how Samson sees them, but in how they lead Samson to see himself. In his encounters with his visitors, Samson comes to regard himself through the surrogate eyes they provide, and the revision of his circumstances that their perspective offers is reflected in a language increasingly more adequate to express the spiritual insight he is moving toward.

As the countrymen whose hopes for deliverance have fled with Samson's defeat, the Chorus anticipates issues raised on a more intimate level with Manoa, but they also represent a simplistic version of Samson's view of himself at the beginning of the poem. To an even greater extent than Samson, the Chorus concentrates on the external, physical aspects of his fall. While he is tortured by the paradoxes of his reversal, however, they simply espouse contradictory positions without attempting to rectify them. Despite their insistence that his previous "high estate" was not due to "long descent of birth / Or the sphere of fortune" (170-172), they locate the cause of his present degradation in the inexplicable turning of Fortune's wheel: "By how much from the top of wondrous glory, / Strongest of mortal men, / To lowest pitch of abject fortune thou art fall'n" (167-169). This failure to perceive the contradiction may be simply a poetic flaw, but it seems to me that their pedestrian expression is integral to the poem, characterizing not only their own limitations but also drawing our attention to an aspect of Samson's personality that they unwittingly help him overcome.

For if the Chorus embraces contradictions without acknowledging them or lectures Samson with theological commonplaces (210-214) in an attempt to fit his fall to the categories of received wisdom, Samson likewise betrays a certain hollowness in his refusal to "call in doubt / Divine Prediction" (43-44) despite his sense that he is disqualified from fulfilling his appointed task. Though they provide him the occasion to unburden himself, to articulate his torment to a commiserating ear, the Chorus shows so little insight into the spiritual causes of his grief that consciously they can only reinforce his reliance upon platitudes. More important than their attempt at consolation, however, is the provocation to self-defense they offer. Faced with their insinuation that he has betrayed his people, Samson is forced to counter in precise terms the common opinion the Chorus echoes. As a result, the absence of conviction he shows in his opening confession of faith changes to vehement certitude. Turning the accusation on them, he reminds them that Israel failed him before he failed Israel; to his victory at Rameth-lechi "Had *Judah* that day join'd, or one whole Tribe, / They had by this possess'd the Towers of *Gath*, / And lorded over them whom now they serve" (265-267).

The arrival of Manoa extends and intensifies the sympathy the Chorus expresses, but his presence also implies an accusation less easily dismissed than theirs. More fully than the Chorus, Manoa shares Samson's awareness of the cruel ironies of his humiliation:

O wherefore did God grant me my request,
And as a blessing with such pomp adorn'd?
Why are his gifts desirable, to tempt
Our earnest Prayers, then, giv'n with solemn hand
As Graces, draw a Scorpion's tail behind?   (356-360)

Though his pain is not as deep as his son's, it is of the same quality and discerns as its cause the same paradoxes which grind Samson's spirit between their terms. Thus in answering Manoa's complaints Samson addresses his own resentment as well, and the fervor of his language reveals a reconciliation to God's justice more complete than his previous submission to "Divine Prediction." But if Samson finds in his father a greater appreciation of his grief than in the Chorus, he also sees both in the topic of their exchange and in Manoa's persistent love a reminder of the heavenly Father whose cause he has abandoned. Rather than comforting Samson, then, Manoa's continued devotion reinforces his son's guilt at having repaid with infidelity the divine solicitude he describes as paternal love:

> I was his nursling once and choice delight,
> His destin'd from the womb,
> Promis'd by Heavenly message twice descending.
> Under his special eye
> Abstemious I grew up and thriv'd amain;
> He led me on to mightiest deeds.   (633-638)

Though Samson can decisively refute the Chorus's accusation that he has failed the Israelites, he can only acquiesce to the charge of betraying God for which Manoa's presence is a tacit reminder. In fact, the defense of God's justice that Manoa elicits forces Samson to feel even more keenly the burden of his guilt, for it leaves him with no extenuating circumstances to plead. Thus if through Manoa Samson is able to purge his resentment, he is nonetheless left at his father's exit with an intensified sense of guilt, and despite its temporary recovery his language again reveals an absence of control that leads him to find his only cure in "death's benumbing Opium" (630). The retrogression seems to be provoked by Manoa's efforts to ransom him. Because the Chorus is more limited in their sympathy, Samson never entirely accepts their definition of his circumstances, and in talking with them he comes to find in his loss of sight a blessing which saves him from realizing the extent of his humiliation. His exchange with Manoa, however, leads him to see himself through his father's eyes, and he recognizes in the offer to ransom him the implication that he has become simply a useless invalid. In treating him so exclusively as an object of pity, Manoa would deprive him even of the bitter dignity of those who suffer justly because they have earned God's anger, and the suggestion leads Samson to consider as the cause of his torment a possibility more horrible than he had previously imagined. Like the Puritans whose condition Samson in some measure represents, he finds the affliction which assures one of God's continued notice far preferable to the "sense of Heav'n's desertion" (632) he feels at Manoa's departure.[8]

If the vision of his son that Manoa offers causes Samson to plunge even more deeply into despair, the image of himself that he imputes to Dalila, while more humiliating, evokes a renewal of energy and intellectual control manifested in the precise reasoning with which he rejects her invitation. Her motives for returning have provoked considerable speculation, but the theories remain unverifiable because Milton has chosen not to clarify her intentions.[9] For the purposes of the poem, all that matters is Samson's interpretation of her motives, and the accuracy or adequacy of his verdict is less significant than how it leads him to see himself. As the flaw she has exhibited in her previous betrayal is "weakness to resist / *Philistian* gold" (830-831), so in her return she shows not love but "furious rage / To satisfy thy lust" (836-837). In refusing Manoa's similar offer Samson has rebelled at being treated as an object of pity; he now rejects along with Dalila the image of himself he imputes to her: an object for physical gratification. She would have him use divine strength, he believes, for the pleasure of a Philistine harlot. To Milton's readers Manoa's continued solicitude may obliquely suggest the constancy, despite appearances, of the heavenly Father's care, and similarly Dalila may provide, in the love she expresses, a parodic analogue to the divine beneficence on which Samson must come to trust. Further, in seeking forgiveness without acknowledging guilt she may imply by omission an important stage in Samson's recovery.[10] Samson, however, cannot know or appreciate patterns of Christian theology which Milton's readers may discover. For him the positive lessons she parodies are less important than the debasing view of himself he imputes to her and banishes along with her. In rejecting her offer he purges himself of the lust to which Rogers attributes Samson's blindness: "[T]he occasion of his sinne was his ungoverned eye, the evill heart being soone inflamed and provoked thereby."[11] But if he overcomes the lust she represents to him, nonetheless he retains the value of seeing himself through her eyes and the detachment thus acquired is reflected in his renewed control of language.

In their exchange he sees himself as having formerly been her toy, and thus it is significant that language, the instrument with which she had earlier defeated him, now becomes the "trivial weapon" he uses to withstand her renewed verbal barrages. As he has with his first wife, Samson has dared to contend with Dalila using words as weapons, and in both instances his hubris has led to his defeat. The answer to his riddle divulged to his wedding guests, he retaliates with arson and forfeits his Timnan bride to the Philistine stake. Similarly he matches wits with Dalila: "Thrice I deluded her, and turn'd to sport / Her importunity, each time perceiving / How openly, and with what impudence / She purpos'd to betray me" (396-399). But on the fourth attempt Samson surrenders his "fort of silence" (236), overpowered "With blandisht parlays, feminine assaults, / Tongue batteries" (403-404). The fullest example in this poem of Satanic rhetoric, Dalila's speech is the instrument whereby she has originally conquered Samson, and her continuing eloquence suggests she is relying upon proven strategy to reassert control over a domain to which she believes she has a right. If her wardrobe is now a comically ineffectual tool for seducing a blind man, nonetheless in speech she remains a "sorceress" (819) whose persuasive power recalls the "fair enchanted cup" of Circe, the "warbling charms" (934) of the Sirens. But Samson has studied the paradoxes of his own life too closely to fall victim again to her sophistry.

Previously Samson has shown himself incapable of learning from the past. Marrying Dalila on the basis of a false analogy with his disastrous first marriage, he then ignores the lessons the perfidy of his Timnan wife and Dalila's earlier betrayals should have taught him. Now, however, he has learned the value of skepticism. While in his bluntness he cannot match the eloquence with which she attempts to regain control of him, nonetheless he is her match in reason, refusing to condone in her a fault he will not forgive in himself and arguing marital obligations against her plea of patriotism. Although in *Paradise Lost* the "mutual accusation" (IX.1187) with which Adam and Eve assail one another is an instance of fallen speech, Samson's incisiveness, like Gabriel's (*PL*, IV.877-967), Christ's, and the Lady's, bears witness to the "Celestial temper" (*PL*, IV.812) of his words. Where with Manoa clarity has fallen victim to despair, Samson's prosecution of Dalila evinces a recovery of verbal power accompanied by a renewal of confidence in his physical strength. Seeking in desperation to circumvent his arguments through an appeal to his former weakness, Dalila attempts to shift their debate to grounds she feels will be more advantageous to her. But the threat of violence with which Samson denies her request suggests he is capable of translating to the physical level the same demolishing force with which he counters her verbal charms.

In his exchange with Dalila, Samson has abandoned his pietistic distrust of language, adopting instead the terse, rational style favored by Restoration linguists. His resort to the precise language of legal distinctions in answering Dalila's arguments, however, precludes an unqualified victory. For while the rigor of his logic may satisfy those readers who share his belief in the superiority of Israelite law, we must recognize that to Dalila his claims must seem less than compelling.[12] Though she admits that his arguments possess an internal logic that hers lack, she denies him ultimate success by refusing to accept the validity of his assumptions. Against Samson's appeal to the sanctity of marriage as the basis for his prosecution, she pleads national security as the overriding motive, and she can flounce off confident that Samson has demonstrated not the falsity of her cause but only the inadequacy of her defense. Just as the paradoxes that beset Samson offer in themselves no means of resolution, the contest of values cannot be decided as long as it is perceived in cultural and legal terms, located along the same temporal, horizontal axis.

Yet if Dalila retires with her dignity unimpaired in her own eyes, Harapha departs "somewhat crestfall'n" (1244). Dalila can retreat into the isolation of her culture assured of her vindication because Samson meets her appeal to a national standard of value with his own reliance upon Israelite law, but he defeats the giant by answering the contingent in terms of the absolute. When Harapha charges him with being "A Murderer, a Revolter, and a Robber" (1180), Samson first mocks the limitations of the law, exploiting its reliance upon observed behavior as the only index to motive. Whatever his intentions, he argues, his actions were blameless until the Philistines provoked him. But the real ground for his defense is not the legal one of provocation but the extralegal one of divine mission: "I was no private but a person rais'd / With strength sufficient and command from Heav'n / To free my country" (1211-1213). Answering this time the categories of human law with the imperatives of divine sanction, Samson shows he has achieved a detachment that allows him to play with legalistic distinctions in a way that confutes and confuses Harapha.

In his confidence in the external and the physical, Harapha personifies the past that haunts Samson. Not only does he represent the enemy Samson has failed to vanquish, he is in his role as successful champion for his people the son Manoa would have preferred, and in his swaggering virility he is the lover Samson believes Dalila wants. But though he conceives of himself as Dagon's champion, Harapha defines his god in terms exclusively legalistic and cultural, and so he is, as Samson calls him, "bulk without spirit vast" (1238). Where Manoa's love is a faltering approximation to its divine counterpart, Dalila's plea for mercy a parodic version of the forgiveness on which Samson must rely, Harapha's relationship to spiritual values is totally negative; he is a summation of all that true heroism is not. In vanquishing the giant Samson does not fully succeed in purging his pride, which is still apparent in his eagerness to appoint the time and place for God to vindicate himself. He does, however, overcome his literalism, preparing himself at last to recognize the spiritual truths to which his experiences have been pointing but which have remained until now hovering just beyond Samson's reach.

To Harapha the difference between Philistines and Israelites is a matter of custom. The Hebrews are to him simply "the unforeskinn'd race" (1100), a phrase recalling the Chorus's synecdochic reference to Samson's felling "A thousand fore-skins" (144) at Rameth-lechi and Samson's equally contemptuous dismissal of his captors as "the uncircumcis'd" (260). Harapha's legalism and literalism are further expounded in his fastidious appeal to the code of chivalry to save him from accepting the challenge of a condemned blind man who "hast need much washing to be toucht" (1107), and in his inability to think symbolically. Accompanying the literalism of primitive cultures is an animism which merges the natural and the super-natural in the magical. Thus for Harapha Samson's strength cannot reside in his hair, "Where strength can least abide, though all thy hairs / Were bristles rang'd like those that ridge the back / Of chaf't wild Boars, or ruffl'd Porcupines" (1136-1138). Instead he attributes Samson's victories to "spells / And black enchantments, some Magician's Art" (1132-1133). Al-though Samson had earlier spoken of his hair as the repository of his might, he now appreciates that its significance lies in its symbolic properties. His "locks unshorn" are to him "The pledge of my unviolated vow" (1143-1144), an interpretation which agrees with William Perkins's reading: "Sampson's strength lay not in his haire (as men commonly think) but because he went out of his calling, by breaking the vow of a Nazarite, when he gave occasion to Dalilah to cut off his haire, therfore he lost his strength."[13]

The capacity to think symbolically requires that we hold the concrete and the abstract levels in suspension, allowing neither the abstract to subsume the concrete (as in allegory) nor the concrete to absorb the transcendent (as in animism). In imputing a symbolic meaning to his hair, Samson demonstrates his growth beyond the self that Harapha represents, a self similarly wedded to legalism and literalism, but it is a growth that Harapha has helped to stimulate. Where Manoa has seen Samson as an object of pity, Dalila (at least as far as Samson is concerned) as an object of lust, Harapha sees him as an object of scorn. Coming to view himself through the eyes of his visitors,

Samson becomes progressively more detached from the limitations his physical circumstances impose. But detachment is only a necessary step toward his renewed heroism, not its substance. Once he transcends the conditions which have seemed a barrier to the fulfillment of God's promise, he can begin to reconcile himself to his present existence in a new way. Thus while previously he has recoiled from the image he finds mirrored in his visitors, here he ironically embraces the prospect of himself as an object of contempt. Taunting Harapha with an aggressively self-deprecating pose, Samson is beginning to regard himself in a new light, preparing himself to discern in his apparent meanness a symbolic potential similar to the one he discovers between his hair and his strength.

Challenging Harapha to single combat, Samson continues the strategy he has used in disputing legal points: he employs a vocabulary familiar to his opponent but applies it in circumstances which make its relevance problematic. In flaunting his meanness Samson allows the giant to refuse combat by appealing to the same code of chivalry in terms of which Samson proposes their duel. Thus by turning on his tormentor paradoxes similar to those that have besieged him earlier in the poem, Samson baffles and humiliates his enemy. But while the disparity between the language of chivalry and the event to which it is applied defeats Harapha, Samson discovers new possibilities in the contrast. The oaken staff with which he proposes to meet the fully armed and armored giant is another of the trivial weapons in Samson's arsenal, looking forward to the sling David will use to dispatch Harapha's son but also recalling and reevaluating the apparently inappropriate instruments Samson has formerly brooded over. As he proposes an unequal battle to decide "whose God is strongest, thine or mine" (1154), Samson seems to realize for the first time the significance of disparity, for by consciously relying upon instruments in themselves trivial, he illustrates the supremacy of God's power. It remains for Samson to explore more fully the implications of the victory his pose has won him, and to refine his ironic language into an instrument capable not only of derision but of affirmation. Perceiving the metaphoric potential latent in his physical attributes, Samson comes to express his vision in a figurative language that asserts his readiness to act in God's service while acknowledging his absolute reliance upon divine strength.

[III]

The development of Samson's character results, with his conquest of Harapha, in a renewed sense of his integrity. Impulsively offering to fight the fully armed giant with only an oaken staff, Samson illustrates the lesson he most needs to learn. Because the power and the victory will belong to God, the triviality of the weapon is immaterial. While Samson seems at this point not to realize the full significance of his gesture, his "rousing motions" (1382) will soon allow him to see himself as a weapon whose triviality does not preclude its effectiveness. But he must first perfect his self-denial, regarding himself, his afflictions, and even his death with indifference, for only in relinquishing his claim to service does he become once more fully serviceable. As the Puritan preacher William Bridge had reminded his congregation, "It's an hard thing for one that hath been used, to be contented to be used no more: oh! that Magistrates, Ministers, Men of service could but be willing to be used no more, and to be laid aside if God will have it so. A man is never more fit for service, then when he is willing to be used no more in service."[14] Thus, still not understanding how both possibilities may eventuate, Samson accompanies the Philistine Officer, confident that the "day will be remarkable," but whether "By some great act, or of my days the last" (1388-1389) he leaves totally to God's disposing.[15]

The blind slave whose degradation had once seemed to invalidate the promise of heroism now acknowledges the possibility of further use. But as his carelessness with words has played a crucial role in his downfall, so now he must not simply perceive but also articulate the terms of his renewal. Like Adam in the last books, Samson has proceeded to clarity by rejecting what is false. Similarly, like the Lady in *Comus* he has responded to the call to salvation, and like Christ in *Paradise Regained* he shows himself ready to answer the call to action. And like all of these, as well as the narrator of *Paradise Lost*, he demonstrates his recovery of the Word through his facility with speech.

Regaining his mastery of language, Samson joins in full equality the company to which he feels his countrymen's fickleness has already entitled him. Among the betrayed Israelite heroes with whom he compares himself is *"Jephtha*, who by argument, / Not worse than by his shield and spear / Defended *Israel* from the *Ammonite*,/. . . In that sore battle when so many died / . . . For want of well pronouncing *Shibboleth"* (283-289). Uniting words and deeds in a way Samson has yet to accomplish, Jephtha defeats his enemies and then, with his pronunciation test, separates the faithful from the hypocrites. Similarly Samson must join victorious deeds to the vanquishing power of the mockery he has directed against Harapha. But more important, he must begin to use language as a means of expressing his sense of the relationship between the divine and the human. The result is at once to confess his submission to God's will and to conceal his meaning from the unfit audience whose literal-mindedness is suitably punished.

Adam reveals his recovery of the inner Word by recognizing the figurative meaning, the latent blessing concealed in God's curse. And the narrator of *Paradise Lost*, like Christ in *Paradise Regained*, responds to God's call by employing a polysemous language of his own. But while the narrator's purpose is to disclose divine truth in a language whose complexity approximates that of its subject, both Samson and Christ use verbal doubleness not just to illuminate a "fit audience" (*PL*, VII.31) but to exclude the unworthy, those who "hearing . . . hear not" (Mt. 13:13). Using puns as Jephtha uses pronunciation, Samson divides his audience between those whose understanding is carnal, idolatrously literal, and those who like Milton's readers are capable of discerning the spiritual references in his speech. The epithet *agonistes* suggests a complex variety of Samson's attributes. His physical athleticism is the most obvious reference, but that in turn points to the spiritual struggle from which he emerges as God's champion, and his physical and spiritual torment resonates as well with the modern sense of the word "agony." But the epithet also indicates his mastery of language. "Agonistic" is a rhetorical term denoting "the attempt to over-come an adversary in argument," a meaning whose relevance is confirmed in Samson's exchanges with Dalila and Harapha.[16] The theatrical applications of the term, however, suggest more fully the nature of Samson's renewed control of words. For Milton the word indicated at once a willing entertainer, an object of ridicule, and a mocking deceiver, and Samson finally subsumes all three possibilities.[17] Not only does he go to the festival in apparent willingness to perform for his captors, he seems almost to encourage their scornful treatment of him by pleading expediency as his motive: "'Masters' commands come with a power resistless / To such as owe them absolute subjec-tion; / And for a life who will not change his purpose?'" (1404-1406). The impulsive flaunting of his meanness which overcomes Harapha has been transformed into a consciously deceptive pose, mocking the Philistines and parodying the Chorus's prudent timidity. The mockery and deception become even more explicit when with devastating irony Samson an-nounces his final demonstration of strength by proclaiming, "Now of my own accord such other trial / I mean to show you of my strength, yet greater / As with amaze shall strike all who behold" (1643-1645). But the language which deceives the Phil-istines as it invites their ridicule or offers to entertain them has for Samson and Milton's readers another dimension. Appa-rently submitting to the threats of his Philistine captors, Samson is in fact acknowledging his obedience to a divine command, and in introducing a new demonstration of his strength ostensibly invented for the diversion of his audience, Samson is actually describing its literally striking effect and at the same time point-ing to the "greater" strength upon which his own depends.

Thus in deceiving the Philistines through language, Samson resumes his earlier role as a riddle-master. But the metaphoric language he speaks both propounds mysteries to the Philistines and expresses his resolution of the riddle of his own life, a resolution based upon his insight into realities comprehended by neither the arrogant bully nor the despairing slave. Like many riddles, the one Samson poses to his wedding guests asks the respondents to reconcile an effect with a cause apparently its opposite: meat from the eater, sweet from the strong. Samson's life has the same "causal contradictive" structure.[18] Somehow he must believe that his degradation does not preclude his heroism just as he has already learned that being God's chosen can result in humiliation. Riddles are not normally amenable to logical inquiry, which only produces the kind of obsessive fascination that draws his visitors to Samson, and Samson to the contradictions between his past and present existences. Instead they require an exercise of intellectual acrobatics: the respondent must maintain a dual perspective, regarding the terms of the puzzle as at once literal and metaphoric until a satisfactory combination of meanings presents itself as a sudden insight.[19]

Just as the solution to Samson's riddle involves juggling the literal and figurative meanings of the terms, so in order to resolve the paradoxes of his life he must discover a significance in God's promise and his present condition not immediately apparent, and in so doing he acquires once more a metaphoric language resembling that of the earlier Samson. Yet the tenor of the metaphors at the end of the poem opens out onto a spiritual dimension not available in his earlier speeches, or in those of Satan and Comus. Like the language with which he seems to acquiesce to his captors' demands, the riddle of the lion and the honey is intended to mock and deceive, but both the vehicle and the tenor of the metaphors in the riddle are drawn from the world of sensory experience. The same constricted imagination is evident in the language with which the biblical Samson accuses his wedding guests: "If you had not plowed with my heifer, you would not have found out my riddle" (Judges 14:18). Similarly Milton's Samson calls Dalila "Monster" (230), "Hyaena" (748), and "viper" (1001), and he likewise turns on himself the scorn these comparisons imply, lamenting that Dalila "shore me / Like a tame Wether" (537-538). Even when Samson refers to God early on, it is in anthropomorphic terms that seem either to reduce God to a jouster (463-471) or to domesticate him into literal fatherhood (633-637). At the end of the poem, however, the metaphors he employs to express his renewed faith in God's guidance, though the vehicles are drawn from human attributes, seem to exalt rather than diminish their divine tenors because they stress not how God is like people but how far his mastery and strength surpass their human analogues. Thus Samson acquires at once the language and the illumination, human words approximating the Word.

Samson's visitors lead him first to transcendence and then, at least incipiently in his challenge to Harapha, to a discovery of his continuing usefulness, and his growing control over words reflects his spiritual convalescence. But the ironic language with which he taunts Harapha has primarily a negative, derisory intent. Achieving a full submission to God's will, he acquires at the same time a metaphoric language capable as well of affirming his faith. This final stage in Samson's development, however, is one for which his visitors provide at best the intellectual form; the substance that underlies his metaphors and seems to confirm his regeneration is supplied inexplicably, attributed to "some rousing motions" (1382). Nothing in his previous experience causes him to understand the relationship between the physical and spiritual dimensions implicit in his figurative speech. Appreciating the tenor of his metaphors requires the possession of special information, available only through internal revelation. Thus if his life assumes the structure of the riddle he poses to his wedding guests, the solution is forthcoming in the same way. For his question is not a true riddle but a "neck" riddle, one on which the riddler may safely risk his neck because its solution depends upon information only he knows.[20] But the knowledge Samson acquires intuitively, through a direct revelation, is accessible to Milton's readers discursively, and his experience assumes greater significance as the result of our familiarity with the Christian theology in terms of whose patterns we define Samson's recovery and his heroism.

As Samson's sudden illumination through the inner Word gives him an advantage over the Philistines and his countrymen, so our possession of the Scriptural Word gives us an advantage over him. Not only do we know the outcome of his trials, we are also aware of the pattern of heroism toward which he is reaching, for we know as Samson does not the antitype whose subsequent actions provide the model for interpreting Samson's regeneration and sacrifice. Aided by the allusion to the Phoenix (1699-1707), we can recognize in Samson's humiliation and martyrdom an anticipation of Christ, a typological resonance made even more pronounced by the imagery of binding and loosing which looks forward to Samson's Christ-like transcendence of Hebrew law. Similarly the parallels between the captivity of the Israelites and the embattled position of the Good Old Cause after the Restoration make Samson an especially appropriate type of the Christian Elect.[21] In a sense, then, the means Samson employs to redefine the heroic potential of his life poses a riddle to Milton's readers, and ours like his depends for its solution on the knowledge only revelation can provide. But where his revelation is special and therefore limited to the circumstances he faces, the revelation to which we have access is general and thus capable of confirming in terms of an accepted pattern not only Samson's regeneration but also its continuing significance to the Church Invisible.

Yet the extent to which our possession of Christian revelation can confirm the divine source of Samson's illumination is limited. Because grace is a free gift registered only in the human soul, we can neither account for its dispensation nor objectively verify its reception with final certainty. Consequently the careful tracing of Samson's regeneration may be no more than a critical myth, an inference of causes from effects such as the one Millicent Bell has performed with *Paradise Lost*.[22] But the absence of conclusive evidence, it seems to me, is not an artistic flaw but a reiteration of one of the poem's basic points. Meaning becomes clear only in retrospect, and while our access to the Scriptural Word seems to confirm the legitimacy of Samson's illumination, nonetheless our interpretation occurs even as God's historical plot continues to unfold, and so we must recognize that our solution is subject to constant revaluation, a process that cannot cease "Till time stand fixt" (*PL*, XII.555). Thus like Samson we must learn to act without knowing fully either the grounds or the consequences of our actions. The confidence of Samson unshorn resides in presumption, the "carnall securitie" that, according to the Puritan John Downame, persists without doubt of salvation, but only so long as "they enjoy the outward benefits of this life."

True assurance, on the other hand, accepts the limits of human certitude as it is marked, in its final stage of sanctification, by not setting "our mindes upon worldly things."[23] Like Samson and Milton's readers, Manoa and the Chorus reinterpret Samson's life from the perspective his martyrdom provides, but lacking revelation their definition of his victory remains confined to the historical and cultural dimensions Samson has come to transcend. Manoa takes grim satisfaction in his son's fulfilling the angel's promise, assuring himself that "*Samson* hath quit himself / Like *Samson*, and heroicly hath finish'd / A life Heroic, on his Enemies / Fully reveng'd hath left them years of mourning, / And lamentation to the Sons of *Caphtor* / Through all *Philistian* bounds" (1709-1714). Yet if we are led to supersede Manoa's response in our knowledge of the typological significance of Samson's martyrdom as well as of the pyrrhic nature of the historical victory Manoa celebrates, we must also acknowledge that his interpretation like ours is based on the best information he has. We must not assume that in our superior knowledge we have measured all the resonances Samson's experience may provide, for the pattern in terms of which we define his experience is still in the process of being fulfilled.

By the end of the poem we are led to realize that language is capable of expressing meanings confined neither to the speaker's intentions nor to the understanding of his auditors. Yet while at the outset Samson takes this polysemous quality of language as a cause for distrust, his development finally reaffirms the metaphoric potential of language as the only means of expressing truths otherwise too complex and apparently contradictory to be apprehended. In the figurative language his "rousing motions" allow him to master, Samson is able to resolve the paradoxes whose disparity had tormented him. The vertical, spiritual dimension he perceives can be joined to the promise of heroism in the horizontal, physical world, and the unity can be expressed, the heroism achieved, through a language capable of referring to both dimensions at once. This convergence of perspectives, then, transforms disjunction to continuity, paradox to metaphor, but as it correspondingly resolves low and high, trivial and ultimate, it generates a language especially appropriate to Christianity, whose central mystery of the Incarnation is itself a sacred pun, a riddle like Samson's concluding speeches. The expression of Samson's heroism, then, reaffirms the language of the poem, which throughout exploits for their metaphoric or typological significance items and events that are otherwise insignificant, suggesting thereby the continuing presence, despite appearances, of God's "guiding hand" (1).

Conclusion

From Babel to Pentecost

THE prevailing conviction about language during the time that Milton was defining his purpose and practicing his art was that words are troublesome, that they tend to obscure or misrepresent the reality for which they stand. Acting upon this conviction, many preachers and theologians urged at the least a style less self-consciously rhetorical than the one typified by Lancelot Andrewes and John Donne. At the extreme, radical Protestants such as the Ranters and Quakers sought to cultivate only the inner voice, arguing that any utterance should flow directly from the spirit without attention to the canons of formal rhetoric. Agreeing with the premise but fearful of the solution, Royal Society philosophers sought instead to purify language through a program of deliberate linguistic reform, eliminating its ambiguities and imprecisions and achieving thereby a verbal system possessing the clarity and accuracy necessary for an instrument of scientific inquiry.

As his tempters and even on occasion his protagonists bear witness, Milton was acutely conscious of the limitations and dangers inherent in words, of their capacity to mislead or deceive. Although the Edenic language of Adam and Eve allows them to express their thoughts and define their physical environment fully and precisely, neither their unfallen vocabulary nor the Book of Nature proves adequate to communicate what they desire to know about God. And if direct revelation is an essential supplement to human speech before the Fall, after their sin Adam and Eve demonstrate a verbal corruption that makes the reliance upon the divine Word even more urgent. The invocation to Book IX, with its stress on the spontaneous, "unpremeditated" production of his epic, underscores Milton's affinity for those radicals who denied the value of any learning or eloquence except that which proceeds without mediation from a divine source.

Yet Milton's verse for the most part provides ample evidence of his deep commitment to learning, and his style typically shows little resemblance either to the vividly direct sobriety of Bunyan or to the mathematically precise language projected by the Royal Society. For while Milton recognized the damage the Fall had inflicted upon human speech, he consistently acknowledged what many of his contemporaries appear to forget, that Babel is balanced by Pentecost, that the *felix culpa* is a concept which extends to language. Following Luther, Calvin, and ultimately Augustine, Milton found illumination to be achieved through an interplay between the divine Word and the spoken or written words of God's ministers and true poets, who can be adequate to their subject only by exploiting all the resources of language at their command. Thus though Original Sin introduced the qualities of confusion and ambiguity into human speech, and Babel made them permanent features of the language, through the Word these attributes are redeemed, their presence adding a dimension to language that permits it to communicate to fallen intellect the complexity, richness, and variety of God's plan.

Throughout his poetry, but particularly in his temptation poems, Milton examines the relationship between the Word and his own art. The protagonists of *Comus* and *Paradise Regained* reveal the Word as it operates prior to the performance of their respective vocational duties, but even there the Lady's speech, like the Son's, clearly derives its power from a divine source. In the exercise of his prophetic mission the narrator of *Paradise Lost* discloses more fully both the operation of the interior Word and its transforming effect on human speech, and at the same time he traces language from its heavenly origins through its Edenic and fallen states and finally to the possibility of its being redeemed for divine use. It is, though, in *Samson Agonistes* that Milton explores with greatest subtlety the dialectic between the inner Word and human language. Although for Samson, as for the Lady and the Son, it is the words of his antagonists and tempters that assist him in clarifying his faith, it is finally a divine intimation that frees him from the Hebraic law and guides him to fulfill his appointed task. Yet the illumination he receives also permits him to resume his earlier identity as a riddler while using his verbal dexterity now not to manifest his pride but to acknowledge his complete submission to God's will. Samson no more than Milton's other protagonists is saved through language, but his heroism like theirs is both expressed and in large measure accomplished through his transformed powers of speech, human words redeemed by the Word of God.

# Notes

Notes

[INTRODUCTION]

1. Henry Cornelius Agrippa, *Of the Vanitie and Uncertaintie of Artes and Sciences*, tr. James Sandford (London, 1569), p. 6.

2. Ibid., pp. 179, 11. For a thorough if controversial treatment of the attacks on literature, see Russell Fraser, *The War Against Poetry* (Princeton, N.J., 1970).

3. Glanvill, *An Essay Concerning Preaching* (London, 1678), pp. 24-25.

4. Sprat, *The History of the Royal-Society of London* (London, 1667), pp. 42-43.

5. My text for the poetry, including translations of the Latin, is *John Milton: Complete Poems and Major Prose*, ed. Merritt Y. Hughes (New York, 1957), and will be cited parenthetically.

6. See Marcia L. Colish, *The Mirror of Language: A Study in the Medieval Theory of Knowledge* (New Haven, Conn., 1968). Colish describes how the concept was interpreted by Augustine, Anselm, Aquinas, and Dante.

7. *The Confessions of St. Augustine*, tr. Rex Warner (New York, 1963), I.1, p. 17.

8. Augustine, *The Trinity*; in *Augustine: Later Works*, tr. John Burnaby (Philadelphia, 1955), IX.12, p. 65.

9. See Augustine, *On Christian Doctrine*, II. xvi.

10. Colish, *The Mirror of Language*, pp. 19-20.

11. Stanley E. Fish, *Self-Consuming Artifacts: The Experience of Seventeenth-Century Literature* (Berkeley, Calif., 1972), pp. 39, 42. See also Joseph Anthony Mazzeo, "St. Augustine's Rhetoric of Silence: Truth vs. Eloquence and Things vs. Signs," in *Renaissance and Seventeenth-Century Studies* (New York, 1964), pp. 1-28. For other treatments of the Word in Milton's poetry, see W.B.C. Watkins, *An Anatomy of Milton's Verse* (Baton Rouge, La., 1955), pp. 42-86; and Georgia B. Christopher, *Milton and the Science of the Saints* (Princeton, N.J., 1982). In *The Paradise Within: Studies in Vaughan, Traherne, and Milton* (New Haven, Conn., 1964), Louis Martz discusses the literary impact of Augustinian patterns of dialectic. More recently, John R. Knott, Jr., has studied some of the more radical Protestant writers and their position on eloquence, like Fish placing Milton's prose in this context; see *The Sword of the Spirit: Puritan Responses to the Bible* (Chicago, 1980).

12. Luther, *The Freedom of a Christian*; in *Luther's Works*, ed. Jaroslav Pelikan and Helmut T. Lehmann, 55 vols. (Philadelphia, 1958-1967), 31: 345. This edition is cited hereafter as "*LW*."

13. Luther, "To the Councilmen of All Cities in Germany That They Establish and Maintain Christian Schools, 1524," *LW*, 45: 360, 362. For a defense of language study as an aid to evangelism, see Luther's preface to "The German Mass and Order of Service, 1526," *LW*, 53: 61-69.

14. John Calvin, *Commentary upon John's Gospel*; in *Calvin's Commentaries*, 45 vols. (Grand Rapids, Mich., 1948-1959), 34: 26. This edition is cited hereafter as *Comm*. Calvin shared with Erasmus a preference for *Sermo* over *Verbum*; see Marjorie O'Rourke Boyle, *Erasmus on Language and Method in Theology* (Toronto, 1977), pp. 3-31.

15. Ronald S. Wallace, *Calvin's Doctrine of the Word and Sacrament* (London, 1953), pp. 90-91.

16. Haller, *The Rise of Puritanism* (New York, 1938), p. 23.

17. Perkins, *The Art of Prophecying*; in *The Workes of . . . W. Perkins*, 3 vols. in 2 (Cambridge, 1608-1609), 2: 759.

18. Haller, *The Rise of Puritanism*, p. 140.

19. Wither, *A Preparation to the Psalter* (London, 1619), p. 67.

20. Ibid., p. 2.

21. Barbara Kiefer Lewalski, *Protestant Poetics and the Seventeenth-Century Religious Lyric* (Princeton, N.J., 1979), pp. 6-7.

22. Whenever possible, quotations from the prose are according to *Complete Prose Works of John Milton*, gen. ed. Don M. Wolfe, 8 vols. (New Haven, 1953-   ), and will be cited parenthetically as "CPW," with volume and page number. Where the Yale edition is not yet available, the source is *The Works of John Milton*, gen. ed. Frank Allen Patterson, 18 vols. in 21 (New York, 1931-1938), identified parenthetically as "CE."

23. See also William Shullenberger, "Linguistic and Poetic Theory in Milton's *De Doctrina Christiana*," *English Language Notes* (hereinafter referred to as *ELN*) 19 (1982): 262-278.

24. For a recent account of the dialectical progress of Milton's thought, see Mary Ann Radzinowicz, *Toward Samson Agonistes: The Growth of Milton's Mind* (Princeton, N.J., 1978).

[CHAPTER ONE]

1. For a discussion of the Diggers in this context, see Knott, *The Sword of the Spirit*, pp. 85-105.

2. Wilkins, *An Essay Towards a Real Character and a Philosophical Language* (London, 1668), p. 21.

3. Sprat, *History of the Royal-Society*, p. 113.

4. Sterry, "The True Orpheus," in *Peter Sterry: Platonist and Puritan*, ed. Vivian de Sola Pinto (Cambridge, 1934), p. 157.

5. John Eachard, *The Grounds and Occasions of the Contempt of the Clergy and Religion Enquired Into*; in *Works* (London, 1705), 11th ed., p. 27; Cowley, "Ode: Of Wit."

6. Anne Davidson Ferry, *Milton's Epic Voice: The Narrator in Paradise Lost* (Cambridge, Mass., 1963), p. 108.

7. Lewis, *A Preface to Paradise Lost* (London, 1942), p. 39ff.

8. For J. B. Broadbent, likewise, the epithets of Heaven and Eden "realise the highest purpose of politeness, to recognise and celebrate the precise nature of the being addressed" (*Some Graver Subject: An Essay on Paradise Lost* [London, 1960], p. 191). See also Kester Svendsen, "Epic Address and Reference and the Principle of Decorum in *Paradise Lost*," *Philological Quarterly* (hereinafter referred to as *PQ*) 28 (1949): 185-206.

9. For the senses of the word "conversation" as Milton uses it, see John Halkett, *Milton and the Idea of Matrimony: A Study of the Divorce Tracts and Paradise Lost* (New Haven, Conn., 1970), p. 58.

10. Jonson, *Timber, or Discoveries* (1641); in *Ben Jonson*, ed. C. H. Herford, Percy and Evelyn Simpson, 11 vols. (Oxford, 1925-1952), 8: 620-621.

11. Stein, *The Art of Presence: The Poet and Paradise Lost* (Berkeley, Calif., 1977), p. 58.

12. Allestree, *The Government of the Tongue* (Oxford, 1674), p. 5.

13. For the Book of Nature as *topos*, see Ernst Robert Curtius, *European Literature and the Latin Middle Ages*, tr. Willard R. Trask (New York, 1953), pp. 319-326.

14. Calvin, *Comm.*, 27: 19.

15. Calvin, *Institutes of the Christian Religion*, ed. John T. McNeill, tr. Ford Lewis Battles (Philadelphia, 1960), IV.xiv.4, p. 1279.

16. This theory of language is given its fullest treatment in Augustine's *De magistro*. The terms "indicative" and "commemorative" are borrowed from Colish, *The Mirror of Language*, p. 5. Calvin's reliance on Augustine in this matter is implicit in much of his writing. Particularly relevant here is Calvin's conviction that "The commonest phenomena of the world are not self-explanatory, and we must rise above them to their Author." See Edward A. Dowey, Jr., *The Knowledge of God in Calvin's Theology* (New York, 1952), p. 75.

17. The sense of divinity is one internal sign of God common to everyone. The other is conscience, the moral sense. See Dowey, *Knowledge of God*, pp. 50-72.

18. Dowey, *Knowledge of God*, p. 108.

19. For the pattern of Augustinian meditation as it was systematized by Bonaventure, see Martz, *The Paradise Within*, p. 54ff.

20. Calvin, *Institutes*, I.i.1, p. 37.

21. For Calvin on the "spectacles" of Scripture, see *Institutes*, I.vi.1 and I.xiv.1.

22. See John E. Parish's treatment of these conversations with God in "Milton and an Anthropomorphic God," *Studies in Philology* (hereinafter referred to as *SP*) 56 (1959): 619-625.

23. Lee A. Jacobus, "Self-Knowledge in *Paradise Lost*: Conscience and Contemplation," *Milton Studies* 3 (1971): 108-116.

24. Puttenham, *The Arte of English Poesie* (London, 1589), p. 4.

25. Schultz, *Milton and Forbidden Knowledge* (New York, 1955), p. 5.

26. Arthur O. Lovejoy, "Milton's Dialogue on Astronomy," in *Reason and the Imagination: Studies in the History of Ideas 1600-1800*, ed. J. A. Mazzeo (New York, 1962), pp. 141-142.

27. Augustine, *Confessions*, V.3, p. 92. For the *scientia/sapientia* distinction, see *City of God*, XIX.1, 3. See also Ronald H. Nash, *The Light of the Mind: St. Augustine's Theory of Knowledge* (Lexington, Ky., 1969), p. 8.

28. See Dowey, *Knowledge of God*, pp. 24-31. Erasmus, "The Epicurean," in *The Colloquies of Erasmus*, tr. Craig R. Thompson (Chicago, 1965), p. 548.

29. Lovejoy, "Milton's Dialogue on Astronomy," p. 140.

30. Augustine, *The Trinity*, XV.16, p. 143.

31. Augustine, *On Christian Doctrine*, tr. D. W. Robertson, Jr. (Indianapolis, Ind., 1958), II.vi, p. 38.

[CHAPTER TWO]

1. South, "The Fatal Imposture, and Force of Words," a sermon on Isaiah 5:20 preached May 9, 1686; in *Twelve Sermons Preached Upon Several Occasions*, 4 vols. (London, 1692-1715), 1: 441.

2. The most significant modern studies in both categories include the following: J. H. Adamson, "The War in Heaven: Milton's Version of the *Merkabah*," *Journal of English and Germanic Philology* (hereinafter referred to as *JEGP*) 57 (1958): 690-703; Anne T. Barbeau, "Satan's Envy of the Son and the Third Day of the War," *Papers on Language and Literature* 13 (1977): 362-371; Boyd M. Berry, *Process of Speech: Puritan Religious Writing and Paradise Lost* (Baltimore, Md., 1976), pp. 170-190; Stanley Eugene Fish, *Surprised by Sin: The Reader in Paradise Lost* (1967; Berkeley, Calif., 1971), pp. 162-196; James A. Freeman, *Milton and the Martial Muse: Paradise Lost and European Traditions of War* (Princeton, N.J., 1980); Roland Mushat Frye, *Milton's Imagery and the Visual Arts: Iconographic Tradition in the Epic Poems* (Princeton, N.J., 1978), pp. 43-64; William B. Hunter, Jr., "Milton on the Exaltation of the Son: The War in Heaven in *Paradise Lost*," *ELH* 36 (1969): 215-231; Michael Lieb, *The Dialectics of Creation: Patterns of Birth and Regeneration in Paradise Lost* (Amherst, Mass., 1970), pp. 81-124; William McQueen, "*Paradise Lost* V, VI: The War in Heaven," *SP* 71 (1974): 89-104; John Peter, *A Critique of Paradise Lost* (New York, 1960), pp. 63-84; Stella P. Revard, "Milton's Critique of Heroic Warfare in *Paradise Lost* V and VI," *Studies in English Literature, 1500-1900* (hereinafter referred to as *SEL*) 7 (1967): 119-139; Revard, "Milton's Gunpowder Poems and Satan's Conspiracy," *Milton Studies* 4 (1972): 63-77; Revard, "The Warring Saints and the Dragon: A Commentary upon Revelation 12:7-9 and Milton's War in Heaven," *PQ* 53 (1974): 181-194; Revard, *The War in Heaven: Paradise Lost and the Tradition of Satan's Rebellion* (Ithaca, N.Y., 1980); William G. Riggs, *The Christian Poet in Paradise Lost* (Berkeley, Calif., 1972), pp. 115-134; Jason P. Rosenblatt, "Structural Unity and Temporal Concordance: The War in Heaven in *Paradise Lost*," *Publications of the Modern Language Association of America* (hereinafter referred to as *PMLA*) 87 (1972): 31-41; Priscilla P. St. George, "Psychomachia in Books V and VI of *Paradise Lost*," *Modern Language Quarterly* (hereinafter referred to as *MLQ*) 27 (1966): 185-196; Arnold Stein, *Answerable Style: Essays on Paradise Lost* (Minneapolis, Minn., 1953), pp. 17-37; Dick Taylor, Jr., "The Battle in Heaven in *Paradise Lost*," *Tulane Studies in English* 3 (1952): 69-92; Stephen Wigler, "Outrageous Noise and the Sovereign Voice: Satan, Sin, and Syntax in *Sonnet XIX* and Book VI of *Paradise Lost*," *Milton Studies* 10 (1977): 155-165; James A. Winn, "Milton on Heroic Warfare," *Yale Review*, ns. 66 (1976-1977): 70-86.

3. Stein, *Answerable Style*, p. 22.

4. See Fish, *Surprised by Sin*, passim.

5. See Stein, *Answerable Style*, p. 29.

6. Luther, *Sermons on the Gospel of St. John: Chapters 1-4*; *LW*, 22: 9.

7. Richard Bentley, *Paradise Lost* (1732), p. 172; Ricks, *Milton's Grand Style* (Oxford, 1963), p. 89.

8. Riggs, *The Christian Poet*, pp. 124-125.

9. Johnson, "Milton," in *The Works of Samuel Johnson Ll.D.*, 11 vols. (1825; rpt. New York, 1970), 7: 136.

10. Landor, *Imaginary Conversations*; in *The Complete Works of Walter Savage Landor*, ed. T. Earle Welby, 16 vols. (London, 1927-1936), 5: 258.

11. Robert H. West, *Milton and the Angels* (Athens, Ga., 1955), p. 92.

12. See Fish, *Surprised by Sin*, pp. 158-207; Berry, *Process of Speech*, pp. 170-190.

13. See Revard, "Milton's Critique of Heroic Warfare," p. 134.

14. Calvin, *Comm.*, 31: 362.

15. Haller, *The Rise of Puritanism*, p. 142.

16. Luther, "To the Councilmen . . . ;" *LW*, 45; 366.

17. Pareus, *A Commentary upon the Divine Revelation of the Apostle and Evangelist John*, tr. Elias Arnold (Amsterdam, 1644), pp. 261, 267.

18. Taylor, *Christs Victorie over the Dragon* (London, 1633), pp. 232, 168, 173, 133, 162. See also Revard, who quotes Stephen Marshall and Jacob Acontius to show the preference for the Word over the sword in Christian warfare (*The War in Heaven*), p. 119.

19. See Joan Webber, *The Eloquent "I": Style and Self in Seventeenth-Century Prose* (Madison, Wisc., 1968), p. 207.

20. Rawlinson, *The Romish Judas* (London, 1611), p. 15.

21. Taylor, *Christs Victorie over the Dragon*, pp. 168, 357. See also Revard, *The War in Heaven*, pp. 86-107.

22. Frye, *Milton's Imagery and the Visual Arts*, pp. 48-49.

23. Augustine, *On Christian Doctrine*, III.v, pp. 83-84.

24. South, "The Fatal Imposture," pp. 458-459.

25. Agrippa, *Vanitie . . . of Artes and Sciences*, p. 18.

26. Josephus, *The Most Auncient Historie of the Jewes*, in *The Famous and Memorable Works of Josephus*, tr. Thomas Lodge (London, 1602), p. 9.

27. Luther, *Luther's Commentary on Genesis*, tr. J. Theodore Mueller, 2 vols. (Grand Rapids, Mich., 1958), 1: 191, 194.

28. Marlowe, *Doctor Faustus* II,ii,108; in *The Complete Plays of Christopher Marlowe*, ed. Irving Ribner (New York, 1963).

29. See Augustine, *Confessions*, Book X.

30. Boehme, *Mysterium Magnum, or An Exposition of the First Book of Moses Called Genesis*, tr. John Sparrow (London, 1654), p. 229. See also Margreta de Grazia, "Shakespeare's View of Language: An Historical Perspective," *Shakespeare Quarterly* 29 (1978): 376.

31. Allestree, *The Government of the Tongue*, p. 7.

32. Anne Davidson Ferry, *Milton and the Miltonic Dryden* (Cambridge, Mass., 1968), p. 57.

33. For the pun on "sapience," see Edward W. Tayler, *Milton's Poetry: Its Development in Time* (Pittsburgh, Pa., 1979), pp. 69, 96.

[CHAPTER THREE]

1. For Adam's insight into the meaning of the *protevangelium*, see Georgia B. Christopher, *Milton and the Science of the Saints*, pp. 163-174.

2. Ferry, *Milton and the Miltonic Dryden*, p. 103.

3. Don Cameron Allen cites the etymology of Clement of Alexandria to show that, in the Hebrew, "if the name of Eve is aspirated it is the same as the feminine of serpent" ("Milton and the Name of Eve," *Modern Language Notes* [hereinafter referred to as *MLN*] 74 [1959]: 682).

4. Johnson, quoted in *Boswell's Life of Johnson*, ed. George Birkbeck Hill rev. by L. F. Powell, 6 vols. (Oxford, 1934), 3: 292.

5. On the insufficiency of the sense of divinity to effect salvation, see Dowey, *Knowledge of God*, p. 50ff. Milton dramatizes this theological point when, in VIII.253-282, he shows Adam asking more questions about the Creator than the Creation is able to answer.

6. For Adam's reaction as an aversion to pain, see Lawrence A. Sasek, "The Drama of *Paradise Lost*, Books XI and XII," rpt. in *Milton: Modern Essays in Criticism*, ed. Arthur E. Barker (New York, 1965), p. 350.

7. For full treatments of the typology of the last books, see Barbara Kiefer Lewalski, "Structure and the Symbolism of Vision in Michael's Prophecy, *Paradise Lost*, Books XI-XII," *PQ* 42 (1963): 25-35; and H. R. MacCallum, "Milton and Sacred History: Books XI and XII of *Paradise Lost*," in *Essays in English Literature from the Renaissance to the Victorian Age Presented to A. S. P. Woodhouse*, ed. Millar MacLure and F. W. Watt (Toronto, 1964), pp. 149-168.

8. See Broadbent, *Some Graver Subject*, p. 276.

9. U. Milo Kaufmann, *The Pilgrim's Progress and Traditions in Puritan Meditation* (New Haven, Conn., 1966), pp. 57-58.

10. For the conceptual nature of typology, see J. Paul Hunter, *The Reluctant Pilgrim: Defoe's Emblematic Method and Quest for Form in Robinson Crusoe* (Baltimore, Md., 1966), p. 102.

11. For discussions of the vision in terms of its contribution to Adam's intellectual and spiritual development, see Sasek, "The Drama of *Paradise Lost*," pp. 342-356, and George Williamson, "The Education of Adam," *MP* 61 (1963-1964): 106-109.

12. Lewalski sees the shift to narrative in Book XII as a way of curbing Adam's sinfully ambitious curiosity, "forcing him to rely with humility and faith upon the revelation of the angel" ("Structure and the Symbolism of Vision," p. 28), but it seems to me that this is a goal substantially achieved by the end of Book XI, before the shift occurs.

13. Augustine, *The City of God*, XV.1, tr. M. Dods, in *Basic Writings of Saint Augustine*, 2 vols., ed. Whitney J. Oates (New York, 1948), 2: 276.

14. Calvin espoused the same principle: "Nature is not only 'order,' but the field of God's special volitions. . . . The *ordo naturae* is simply *the orderliness or constancy of God's will within nature*. This is not an empirical orderliness pure and simple, but an order such that God can work miracles, which are a scandal from the point of view of empirical order, without breaking the order of nature" (Dowey, *Knowledge of God*, pp. 66-67; emphasis his).

15. Lewis, *Preface*, pp. 125-126. Lewis's criticism has stimulated a number of incisive responses. These include, in addition to essays cited elsewhere, F. T.

Prince, "On the Last Two Books of *Paradise Lost*," *Essays and Studies*, ns. 11 (1958): 38-52; George Wesley Whiting, *Milton and This Pendant World* (Austin, Tex., 1958), pp. 172-191; and most recently, Raymond B. Waddington, "The Death of Adam: Vision and Voice in Books XI and XII of *Paradise Lost*," *MP* 70 (1972-1973): 9-21. Most of these essays are addressed to the question of structure, demonstrating the existence of a number of patterns—theological, typological, and psychological—where Lewis found none. My own effort is a response to the question of style, relating the shifts in method and medium to Michael's search for an appropriate way to convey the divine message to Adam's fallen mind.

16. Haller, *The Rise of Puritanism*, pp. 108, 101.

17. For a succinct treatment of the issues involved in the quarrel, see D. J. Gordon, "Poet and Architect: The Intellectual Setting of the Quarrel Between Ben Jonson and Inigo Jones," *Journal of the Warburg and Courtauld Institutes* 12 (1949): 152-178. A more recent discussion may be found in Angus Fletcher, *The Transcendental Masque: An Essay on Milton's Comus* (Ithaca, N.Y., 1971), pp. 87-115.

18. Martz, *The Paradise Within*, pp. 150-151. For another response to Martz, see Arnold Stein, "The Paradise Within and the Paradise Without," *MLQ* 26 (1965): 597-600.

19. Boehme, *Mysterium Magnum*, p. 233. Luther, *Commentary on Genesis*, 1: 191.

20. Boehme, *Mysterium Magnum*, p. 233.

21. Calvin, *Comm.*, 36: 75.

22. Luther, "The German Mass and Order of Service, 1526," *LW*, 53: 63.

[CHAPTER FOUR]

1. The seminal studies in this line are A.S.P. Woodhouse, "The Argument of Milton's *Comus*," *University of Toronto Quarterly* (hereinafter referred to as *UTQ*) 11 (1941-1942): 46-71, and "*Comus* Once More," *UTQ* 19 (1949-1950): 218-223. Pursuing Woodhouse's lead are William G. Madsen, "The Idea of Nature in Milton's Poetry," in *Three Studies in the Renaissance: Sidney, Jonson, Milton* (New Haven, Conn., 1958), pp. 181-283; James G. Taaffe, "Michael-mas, the 'Lawless Hour,' and the Occasion of Milton's *Comus*," *ELN* 6 (1968-1969): 257-262; and William B. Hunter, Jr., "The Liturgical Context of *Comus*," *ELN* 10 (1972-1973): 11-15. Readings based on a more rigorous Protestantism have been advanced, however. William Haller asserts, "*Comus* and *Lycidas* are as authentic expressions of the Puritan spirit on the eve of the revolution as anything that came from the hand of Prynne" (*The Rise of Puritanism*, p. 317). For more recent Puritan interpretations, see Alice-Lyle Scoufos, "The Mysteries in Milton's *Masque*," *Milton Studies* 6 (1974): 113-142; and Georgia B. Christopher, "The Virginity of Faith: *Comus* as a Reformation Conceit," *ELH* 43 (1976): 479-499.

2. Perkins, *A Commentarie . . . upon . . . Galatians*; *Workes*, 2: 205. See also Jackson Campbell Boswell, "Milton and Prevenient Grace," *SEL* 7 (1967): 83-94.

3. Calvin, *Institutes*, III.vii.7, p. 697.

4. See Augustine, *Confessions*, Book X.8-26.

5. See John G. Demaray, *Milton and the Masque Tradition: The Early Poems, "Arcades," and Comus* (Cambridge, Mass., 1968), p. 93; and also Madsen, "The Idea of Nature," p. 213.

6. Christopher, *Milton and the Science of the Saints*, p. 43.

7. Calvin, *Institutes*, III.vii.1, pp. 689-690. See also Milton, *Christian Doctrine*, I.xxi.

8. Augustine, *Confessions*, VII.7-21.

9. Perkins, *A Treatise of the Vocations; Workes*, 1: 729.

10. See John Spencer Hill, *John Milton: Poet, Priest, and Prophet: A Study of Divine Vocation in Milton's Poetry and Prose* (London, 1979), p. 15.

11. Perkins, *A Treatise of the Vocations; Workes*, 1: 727.

12. Calvin, *Institutes*, III.x.6, p. 724.

13. Hill, *John Milton*, pp. 192-193.

14. For Christ's fulfillment of these roles, see Barbara Kiefer Lewalski, *Milton's Brief Epic: The Genre, Meaning, and Art of Paradise Regained* (Providence, R.I., 1966), pp. 164-321.

15. For the doctrine of stewardship in *Comus*, see Christopher, "The Virginity of Faith," p. 491.

16. Luther, "Notes on Ecclesiastes;" *LW*, 15: 152.

17. Perkins, *A Declaration of Certaine Spiritual Desertions; Workes*, 1: 415. *A Treatise of the Vocations; Workes*, 1: 743.

18. Luther, "Notes on Ecclesiastes;" *LW*, 15: 49.

19. Perkins, *A Treatise of the Vocations; Workes*, 1: 738.

20. Ibid.

21. Wilson, *Selfe Deniall, or A Christians Hardest Taske* (London, 1625), p. 5.

22. Taylor, *Christs Combate and Conquest* (Cambridge, 1618), pp. 75-76.

23. For an elaboration of this point, see Lee Sheridan Cox, "Food-Word Imagery in *Paradise Regained*," *ELH* 28 (1961): 225-243.

24. Perkins, *The Combate betweene Christ and the Devill Displayed; Workes*, 3: 384.

25. See Michael Fixler, "The Unclean Meats of the Mosaic Law and the Banquet Scene in *Paradise Regained*," *MLN* 70 (1955): 573-577.

26. Baxter, *A Treatise of Self-Denyall* (London, 1660), p. 239.

27. Schultz, "Christ and Antichrist in *Paradise Regained*," *PMLA* 67 (1952): 790-808.

28. Dowey, *Knowledge of God*, pp. 84-85.

29. Ibid., p. 85.

30. See Dick Taylor, Jr., "The Storm Scene in *Paradise Regained*: A Reinterpretation," *UTQ* 24 (1954-1955): 360.

31. Wallace, *Word and Sacrament*, p. 74.

32. See, for instance, Edward Cleveland, "On the Identity Motive in *Paradise Regained*," *MLQ* 16 (1955): 235.

33. Willet, *An Harmonie upon the First Booke of Samuel* (Cambridge, 1607), p. 32.

34. Fish, "Inaction and Silence: The Reader in *Paradise Regained*," in *Calm of Mind: Tercentenary Essays on Paradise Regained and Samson Agonistes in Honor of John S. Diekhoff*, ed. J. A. Wittreich, Jr. (Cleveland, Ohio, 1971), p. 43.

35. Baxter, *Certain Disputations of Right to Sacraments and the True Nature of Visible Christianity* (London, 1658), p. 474.

36. Nicolson, *John Milton: A Reader's Guide to His Poetry* (New York, 1963), p. 326. Louis L. Martz, in "*Paradise Regained*: The Meditative Combat" (*ELH*

27 [1960]: 223-247), finds the model in Virgil's *Georgics*; Lewalski, in *Milton's Brief Epic*, argues for the Book of Job.

37. Fish, "Inaction and Silence," passim.

[CHAPTER FIVE]

1. Luther, *The Freedom of a Christian*; *LW*, 31: 361.

2. For the association of chastity and poetry in Milton, see John M. Steadman, "Chaste Muse and 'Casta Juventus': Milton, Minturno, and Scaliger on Inspiration and the Poet's Character," *Italica* 40 (1963): 28-34; Sheridan D. Blau, "Milton's Salvational Aesthetic," *Journal of Religion* 46 (1966): 288; and Edward Tayler, *Milton's Poetry*, pp. 137-140. The former places Milton's attitude in the context of Italian theories of inspiration, the two latter of Christian ethics.

3. Augustine, *Christian Doctrine*, IV.xxvii, p. 164.

4. Augustine, *Confessions*, VI.2, p. 113.

5. Mazzeo, "St. Augustine's Rhetoric of Silence," p. 17.

6. Perkins, *Art of Prophecying*; *Workes*, 2: 760.

7. Calvin, *Comm.*, 31: 364-365. See also H. Jackson Forstman, *Word and Spirit: Calvin's Doctrine of Biblical Authority* (Stanford, Calif., 1962), pp. 80-84.

8. Baxter, *A Treatise of Conversion* (London, 1658), p. 93.

9. See Larzer Ziff, "The Literary Consequences of Puritanism," *ELH* 30 (1963): pp. 298-299.

10. Rogers, *A Commentary upon the Whole Booke of Judges* (London, 1615), p. 349.

11. Sterry, "The Book of God," *Peter Sterry*, p. 156.

12. Wither, *A Preparation to the Psalter*, p. 38.

13. Sidney, "An Apology for Poetry" (c.1583); in *English Literary Criticism: The Renaissance*, ed. O. B. Hardison, Jr. (New York, 1963), p. 104. See also S. K. Heninger, Jr., "Sidney and Milton: The Poet as Maker," in *Milton and the Line of Vision*, ed. Joseph Anthony Wittreich, Jr. (Madison, Wisc., 1975), pp. 57-95.

14. See Augustine, *De musica*, I.iv. See also William Kerrigan, *The Prophetic Milton* (Charlottesville, Va., 1974), p. 147; and Emmanuel Chapman, *Saint Augustine's Philosophy of Beauty* (New York, 1939), p. 76.

15. Bunyan, *Grace Abounding to the Chief of Sinners*, ed. Roger Sharrock (Oxford, 1966), p. 5. For the sake of consistency I have retained Bunyan's emphases by reversing his usage of italics.

16. Donne, *Devotions upon Emergent Occasions*, ed. Anthony Raspa (Montreal, 1975), Exp. 19, p. 99.

17. The most notable argument for the colloquy as drama is Irene Samuel's, "The Dialogue in Heaven: A Reconsideration of *Paradise Lost*, III, 1-417," *PMLA* 72 (1957): 601-611. C. A. Patrides has eloquently advanced the "subordinationist" position in "The Godhead in *Paradise Lost*: Dogma or Drama?" *JEGP* 64 (1965): 29-34. Jackson I. Cope, on the other hand, argues for the ritualistic character of the episode, in *The Metaphoric Structure of Paradise Lost* (Baltimore, Md., 1962), pp. 164-176. See also Merritt Y. Hughes, "The

Filiations of Milton's Celestial Dialogue," *Ten Perspectives on Milton* (New Haven, Conn., 1965), pp. 104-135; and Isabel G. MacCaffrey, "The Theme of *Paradise Lost*, Book III," in *New Essays on Paradise Lost*, ed. Thomas Kranidas (Berkeley, Calif., 1969), pp. 58-85.

18. Sir Henry Vane, *The Retired Mans Meditations, or, The Mysterie and Power of Godlines* (London, 1655), pp. 2, 1-2.

19. Luther, *Sermons on the Gospel of St. John: Chapters 1-4, LW*, 22: 28-29.

20. See also Joseph H. Summers, *The Muse's Method: An Introduction to Paradise Lost* (Cambridge, Mass., 1962), p. 95; and W.B.C. Watkins, who observes, "Motion Milton identifies with life itself" (*An Anatomy of Milton's Verse*, p. 58).

21. See Ferry, *Milton's Epic Voice*, pp. 131-133.

22. Augustine, *Confessions*, II.6, p. 48.

23. Luther, *Lectures on Romans, LW*, 25: 346. Georgia Christopher has shown how Luther's characterization of sin as curved in on itself stands behind the Elder Brother's conviction in *Comus* that "evil on itself shall back recoil . . . Self-fed and self-consum'd" (593-597); see *Milton and the Science of the Saints*, pp. 36, 96.

24. Cowley, "Preface" to *Poems* (1656); in *The Works of Mr Abraham Cowley* (London, 1668), n.p. See also James H. Sims, "Milton, Literature as a Bible, and the Bible as Literature," in *Milton and the Art of Sacred Song*, ed. J. Max Patrick and Roger H. Sundell (Madison, Wisc., 1979), pp. 20-21.

25. Sprat, *History of the Royal-Society*, p. 111.

26. Smith, "Of Prophecy," in *Select Discourses* (London, 1660), p. 197.

27. Fish, *Surprised by Sin*, passim.

28. Lewis, *Preface*, p. 44.

29. Brisman, *Milton's Poetry of Choice and Its Romantic Heirs* (Ithaca, N.Y., 1973), p. 76.

30. Lewalski, "Time and History in *Paradise Regained*," in *The Prison and the Pinnacle*, ed. Balachandra Rajan (Toronto, 1973), pp. 69, 77.

[CHAPTER SIX]

1. For a recent treatment of *Samson Agonistes* as a culmination of other patterns, see Radzinowicz, *Toward Samson Agonistes*.

2. Ferry, *Milton and the Miltonic Dryden*, p. 177. See also Marcia Landy, "Language and the Seal of Silence in *Samson Agonistes*," *Milton Studies* 2 (1970): 175-194; and the brief rejoinder to both by Anthony Low, *The Blaze of Noon: A Reading of Samson Agonistes* (New York, 1974), pp. 107-108. Low points out that Ferry and Landy overstate their case, basing their argument for the whole poem on an attitude expressed by Samson prior to his final illumination. He does not, however, explore the significance of Samson's recovery of deceptive language, finding the irony of his last speeches to be the result simply of "tactical necessity" (p. 107).

3. Johnson, *The Rambler*, No. 140; in *The Yale Edition of the Works of Samuel Johnson*, Vol. 4, ed. W. J. Bate and Albrecht B. Strauss (New Haven, Conn., 1969), p. 379.

4. Marshall, *Gods Master-piece* (London, 1645), p. 10.

5. Rogers, *Commentary*, pp. 365, 614.

6. For a full treatment of purgation, see Raymond B. Waddington, "Melancholy Against Melancholy: *Samson Agonistes* as Renaissance Tragedy," in *Calm of Mind*, pp. 259-287. Although my discussion, like Waddington's, follows what seems to be a consensus, there is far from general agreement on the specific fault each visitor represents. Sherman H. Hawkins, for instance, sees Samson purging the tragic passions grief, pity, and fear ("Samson's Catharsis," *Milton Studies* 2 [1970]: 223); while Georgia Christopher finds his visitors purging Samson of rage against God, search for extenuation, and fastidiousness ("Homeopathic Physic and Natural Renovation in *Samson Agonistes*," *ELH* 37 [1970]: 361-373); and Radzinowicz sees him facing self-doubt in the Chorus, self-tenderness in Manoa, appetency in Dalila, and aggression in Harapha (*Toward Samson Agonistes*, p. 52). Other critics prefer to demarcate Samson's development in theological terms. See, for instance, John M. Steadman, " 'Faithful Champion': The Theological Basis of Milton's Hero of Faith," *Anglia* 77 (1959): 12-28; and George M. Muldrow, *Milton and the Drama of the Soul: A Study of the Theme of the Restoration of Men in Milton's Later Poetry* (The Hague, 1970), pp. 170-225.

7. For the terms of the disagreement, see Paul R. Sellin, "Sources of Milton's Catharsis: A Reconsideration," *JEGP* 60 (1961): 712-730; Martin Mueller, "Sixteenth-Century Italian Criticism and Milton's Theory of Catharsis," *SEL* 6 (1966): 139-150; and Radzinowicz, *Toward Samson Agonistes*, pp. 55-66.

8. Interpreting afflictions as a sign of God's solicitude is not limited to Puritanism, but it is a view Puritans after the Restoration found especially congenial.

9. Most critics, agreeing with Thomas Kranidas that "Dalila's speeches show her as too clever, too easily various to be simply lecherous" ("Dalila's Role in *Samson Agonistes*," *SEL* 6 [1966]: 136), follow Joseph H. Summers in finding in her "the prototype of the woman who wishes to reduce her lover to an object totally within her power" ("The Movements of the Drama," in *The Lyric and Dramatic Milton*, ed. Summers [New York, 1965], p. 167). Similarly, A. B. Chambers sees her impelled by *malitia*, "a perverse love of causing harm" ("Wisdom and Fortitude in *Samson Agonistes*," *PMLA* 78 [1963]: 318). On the other hand, William Empson accepts her reasons ("A Defense of Delilah," *Sewanee Review* 68 [1960]: 240-255); and Don Cameron Allen agrees, but only because she is too shallow to recognize in herself the motives Samson detects (*The Harmonious Vision*, pp. 88-89).

10. For this reading of Manoa, see Nancy Y. Hoffman, "Samson's Other Father: The Character of Manoa in *Samson Agonistes*," *Milton Studies* 2 (1970): 195-210. For the spiritual resonances of the Dalila episode, see Radzinowicz, "Eve and Dalila: Renovation and the Hardening of the Heart," in *Reason and the Imagination*, pp. 155-181; Charles Mitchell, "Dalila's Return: The Importance of Pardon," *College English* 26 (1964-1965): 614-620; Heather Asals, "In Defense of Dalila: *Samson Agonistes* and the Reformation Theology of the Word," *JEGP* 74 (1975): 183-194; and Joyce Colony, "An Argument for Milton's Dalila," *Yale Review* ns. 66 (1976-1977): 562-575.

11. Rogers, *Commentary*, p. 730.

12. At least two critics have argued that the debate remains unresolved: Virginia R. Mollenkott, "Relativism in *Samson Agonistes*," *SP* 67 (1970): 89-102;

and Stanley Fish, "Question and Answer in *Samson Agonistes*," *Critical Quarterly* 11 (1969): 237-264. For a recent attack on this position which finds Samson's arguments wholly persuasive, see Joan S. Bennett, " 'A Person Rais'd: Public and Private Cause in *Samson Agonistes*," *SEL* 18 (1978): 155-168. While the legal distinctions Bennett draws may be valid, they can only be effective refutations if Dalila accepts their legality, which she does not. Robert H. West also questions relativistic interpretations, in "Samson's God: 'Beastly Hebraism' and 'Asinine Bigotry,' " *Milton Studies* 13 (1979): 109-128.

13. Perkins, *A Treatise of the Vocations*; *Workes*, 1: 729.

14. Bridge, *England Saved with a Notwithstanding* (London, 1648), p. 22.

15. This future reconciliation of apparent opposites Low calls the "irony of alternatives." He finds it pervasive in *Samson Agonistes* and, with one exception, unique to Milton's poem (pp. 77-89).

16. See Alan Rudrum, *A Critical Commentary on Milton's 'Samson Agonistes'* (London, 1969), p. 18.

17. See Paul R. Sellin, "Milton's Epithet *Agonistes*," *SEL* 4 (1964): 145-146.

18. The terminology is borrowed from Robert A. Georges and Alan Dundes, "Toward a Structural Definition of the Riddle," *Journal of American Folklore* 76 (1963): 115-116.

19. For the "flash of recognition" which produces the solution to riddles, see Roger D. Abrahams and Alan Dundes, "Riddles," in *Folklore and Folklife: An Introduction*, ed. Richard M. Dorson (Chicago, 1972), p. 130.

20. For Samson's question as a neck riddle, see Archer Taylor, "The Varieties of Riddles," in *Philologica: The Malone Anniversary Studies*, ed. Thomas A. Kirby and Henry Bosley Woolf (Baltimore, Md., 1949), p. 6.

21. For the equation of *electus* with *sanctus* in the Samson story, see F. Michael Krouse, *Milton's Samson and the Christian Tradition* (Princeton, N.J., 1949), p. 30. Barbara Lewalski also discusses Samson as a type of the Christian Elect, in "*Samson Agonistes* and the 'Tragedy' of the Apocalypse," *PMLA* 85 (1970): 1055.

22. Bell, "The Fallacy of the Fall in *Paradise Lost*," *PMLA* 68 (1953): 863-883. For the suggestion that no regeneration occurs, see E.M.W. Tillyard, who argues that Samson is regenerate throughout (*Milton* [1930; rev. ed., London, 1966], p. 286), and G. A. Wilkes, who questions whether Samson's regeneration is complete even after his encounter with Harapha ("The Interpretation of *Samson Agonistes*," *Huntington Library Quarterly* 26 [1962-1963]: 372-375). See also Irene Samuel, "*Samson Agonistes* as Tragedy," in *Calm of Mind*, pp. 250-257; and Fish, "Question and Answer," p. 252.

23. Downame, *The Christian Warfare* (London, 1604), pp. 222-223, 229.

Index

Abrahams, Roger D., 184
Acontius, Jacob, 177
Adamson, J. H., 176
Agrippa, Henry Cornelius, 2, 3, 4, 14, 62, 173, 177
Allen, Don Cameron, 178, 183
Allestree, Richard, 25-26, 69, 175, 177
Ambrose, Saint, 8, 9
Andrewes, Lancelot, 116, 168
Anselm, Saint, 173
Aquinas, Saint Thomas, 173
Arianism, 128
Aristotle, 7
Arnold, Elias, 177
Asals, Heather, 183
Augustine, Saint, 8-11, 12, 30, 38, 50, 58-59, 84, 137, 169, 173, 175, 176, 177, 178, 179, 180, 181, 182
  Ciceronian training of, 2
  eloquence of example in, 122
  dialectic in, 10
  on *ænigma*, 41
  on art, 125-126, 127
  on Bible, 121
  on dualism, 99
  on memory, 65
  on signs, 29

Babel, Tower of, 1, 2, 19, 62, 69, 88-89, 90, 169
Bacon, Sir Francis, 7, 37-38
Barbeau, Anne T., 176
Barker, Arthur E., 178
Bate, W. J., 182
Battles, Ford Lewis, 175
Baxter, Richard, 86, 116-117, 123, 180, 181

Bell, Millicent, 165, 184
Bennett, Joan S., 184
Bentley, Richard, 49, 58, 117
Berry, Boyd M., 176, 177
Bible, 11, 13, 30, 121, 138 (*see also* Scripture)
Blau, Sheridan D., 181
Boehme, Jacob, 69, 88, 89, 177, 179
Bonaventure, Saint, 175
Boswell, Jackson Campbell, 179
Boyle, Marjorie O'Rourke, 174
Bridge, William, 160, 184
Bridgewater, Earl of, 101-102
Brisman, Leslie, 141-142, 182
Broadbent, J. B., 175, 178
Bunyan, John, 57, 126-127, 169, 181
Buonmattei, Benedetto, 17
Burnaby, John, 173
Butler, Samuel, 5, 6

Callot, Jacques, 58
Calvin, John, 2, 16, 30, 31, 55, 89, 123, 169, 174, 175, 177, 178, 179, 180, 181
  epistemology of, 29
  knowledge of God in, 12, 40
  on calling, 101
  on intention, 94
  on natural theology, 28, 79, 92-93, 113
  on sacraments, 12, 114
  on self-denial, 98
  on works, 120
Chambers, A. B., 183
Chapman, Emmanuel, 181
Charles I, King, 1, 63
Charles II, King, 43
Chaucer, Geoffrey, 5

Christopher, Georgia B., 173, 178, 179, 180, 182, 183
Cicero, 2, 3, 41
Clement of Alexandria, 178
Cleveland, Edward, 180
Colish, Marcia L., 10, 173, 175
Colony, Joyce, 183
Cope, Jackson I., 181
Copernicus, Nicholas, 37, 42
Cowley, Abraham, 23, 138, 174, 182
Cox, Lee Sheridan, 180
Curtius, Ernst Robert, 175

Dante Alighieri, 120, 173
de Grazia, Margreta, 177
Dell, William, 4
Demaray, John G., 180
Descartes, René, 6, 37
Diggers, 21, 174
Dods, M., 178
Donne, John, 41, 126-127, 133, 168, 181
Dorson, Richard M., 184
Dowey, Edward A., 30, 113, 175, 176, 178, 180
Downame, John, 165, 184
Dundes, Alan, 184

Eachard, John, 23, 174
Eliot, T. S., 141
Empson, William, 183
Erasmus, Desiderius, 40, 174, 176

Fawkes, Guy, 57-58
Ferry, Anne Davidson, 69, 75, 146, 174, 177, 178, 182
Fish, Stanley E., 10, 116, 117, 140-141, 173, 176, 177, 180, 181, 182, 184
Forstman, H. Jackson, 181
Fraser, Russell, 173
Freeman, James A., 176
Frye, Roland, 58, 176, 177

Georges, Robert A., 184
Glanvill, Joseph, 4-5, 173
Gordon, D. J., 179
Halkett, John, 175

Haller, William, 14, 55, 86, 174, 177, 179
Hardison, O. B., Jr., 181
Hawkins, Sherman H., 183
Heninger, S. K., Jr., 181
Herbert, George, 15, 36, 38, 51
Hill, George Birkbeck, 178
Hill, John Spencer, 102, 180
Hoffman, Nancy Y., 183
Holy Spirit, 4, 13, 105
Hooker, Richard, 27
Hunter, J. Paul, 178
Hunter, William B., Jr., 176, 179
Hughes, Merritt Y., 173, 181-182

Incarnation, 74, 167 (*see also* Word, Incarnate)
Interior Teacher, 74 (*see also* Word, inner)

Jacobus, Lee A., 34, 175
James I, King, 1, 57
Johnson, Samuel, 51, 76, 149, 177, 178, 182
Jones, Inigo, 63, 87
Jonson, Ben, 7, 24, 63, 87, 175
Josephus, Flavius, 62, 177

Kaufmann, U. Milo, 80, 178
Kerrigan, William, 181
Kirby, Thomas A., 184
Knott, John R., Jr., 173, 174
Kranidas, Thomas, 182, 183
Krouse, F. Michael, 184

Landor, Walter Savage, 52-53, 177
Landy, Marcia, 182
Lehmann, Helmut T., 173
Lewalski, Barbara Kiefer, 15, 117, 143, 174, 178, 180, 181, 182, 184
Lewis, C. S., 23-24, 85-86, 141, 174, 178-179, 182
Lieb, Michael, 176
Lodge, Thomas, 177
Logos, 8, 12, 13, 16, 32 (*see also* Word)
Lovejoy, Arthur O., 36, 37, 40-41, 175, 176

Low, Anthony, 182, 184
Luther, Martin, 2, 10-12, 17, 56, 62,
    88-89, 94, 105, 137, 169, 173,
    174, 177, 179, 180, 181, 182
  on inner Word, 47-48
  on works, 104, 120, 121

MacCaffrey, Isabel G., 182
MacCallum, H. R., 178
MacLure, Millar, 178
McNeill, John T., 175
McQueen, William, 176
Madsen, William G., 179, 180
Marlowe, Christopher, 62-63, 177
Marshall, Stephen, 149, 177, 182
Martz, Louis L., 88, 117, 173, 175,
    179, 180-181
Marvell, Andrew, 33
Mazzeo, J. A., 122, 173, 175, 181
Mitchell, Charles, 183
Mollenkott, Virginia R., 183
More, Henry, 53
Mueller, J. Theodore, 177
Mueller, Martin, 183
Muldrow, George M., 183

Nash, Ronald H., 175
Nicolson, Marjorie, 117, 180
Nimrod, 62, 88

Oates, Whitney J., 178
Oedipus, 150

Pareus, David, 56-57, 177
Parish, John E., 175
Patrick, J. Marx, 182
Patrides, C. A., 181
Patterson, Frank Allen, 174
Paul, Saint, 41, 56, 113
Pelikan, Jaroslav, 173
Pentecost, 19, 28, 88-89, 90, 169
Perkins, William, 14, 122-123, 158,
    174, 179, 180, 181, 184
  on calling, 100-101, 105
  on grace, 94
  on Scriptural Word, 107
  on work, 104
Peter, John, 176

Petrarch, 120
Pinto, Vivian de Sola, 174
Plato, 7, 120
Pope, Alexander, 7, 127
Powell, L. F., 178
Prince, F. T., 178-179
Prynne, William, 3, 179
Ptolemy, 37, 42
Puttenham, George, 35, 175

Quakers, 4, 168
Quintilian, 3

Radzinowicz, Mary Ann, 174, 182,
    183
Rajan, Balachandra, 182
Ranters, 4, 168
Raspa, Anthony, 181
Rawlinson, John, 57-58, 177
Revard, Stella P., 176, 177
Ribner, Irving, 177
Ricks, Christopher, 49, 177
Riggs, William G., 50, 176, 177
Robertson, D. W., Jr., 176
Rogers, Richard, 124, 149-150, 155,
    181, 182, 183
Rosenblatt, Jason P., 176
Royal Society, 4-5, 6, 7, 15, 21, 22,
    168, 169
Rudrum, Alan, 184

St. George, Priscilla P., 176
Samuel, Irene, 181, 184
Sanford, James, 173
Sasek, Lawrence A., 178
Schultz, Howard, 36, 175, 180
Scoufos, Alice-Lyle, 179
Scripture, 2, 4, 9, 10, 11, 12, 13, 29,
    30, 31, 41, 56, 74, 79, 103, 107,
    111, 114, 116, 122, 135, 138,
    139, 175
Sellin, Paul R., 183, 184
Sharrock, Roger, 181
Shullenberger, William, 174
Sidney, Sir Philip, 15, 86, 125, 136,
    181
Simpson, Percy and Evelyn, 175
Sims, James H., 182

Smith, John, 140, 182
South, Robert, 43, 61-62, 176, 177
Sparrow, John, 177
Spenser, Edmund, 108
Sprat, Thomas, 5-6, 22, 139, 173, 174, 182
Steadman, John M., 181, 183
Stein, Arnold, 24, 44, 175, 176, 177, 179
Sterry, Peter, 22, 34, 125, 174, 181
Strauss, Albrecht B., 182
Summers, Joseph H., 182, 183
Sundell, Roger H., 182
Svendsen, Kester, 175

Taaffe, James G., 179
Tayler, Edward W., 177, 181
Taylor, Archer, 184
Taylor, Dick, Jr., 176, 180
Taylor, Thomas, 57, 58, 105-106, 177, 180
Thompson, Craig R., 176
Tillyard, E. M. W., 184
Trask, Willard R., 175

Vane, Sir Henry, 129, 182
Virgil, 117, 181

Waddington, Raymond B., 179, 183
Wallace, Ronald S., 12, 174, 180
Warner, Rex, 173
Watkins, W. B. C., 173, 182
Webber, Joan, 177
Welby, T. Earle, 177
West, Robert H., 53, 177, 184
Whiting, George Wesley, 179

Wigler, Stephen, 176
Wilkes, G. A., 184
Wilkins, John, 22, 174
Willet, Andrew, 115, 180
Williamson, George, 178
Wilson, Christopher, 105, 180
Winn, James A., 176
Wither, George, 14-15, 125, 174, 181
Wittreich, Joseph Anthony, Jr., 180, 181
Wolfe, Don M., 174
Woodhouse, A. S. P., 179
Woolf, Henry Bosley, 184
Word, 2, 11, 13, 18, 19, 22, 26, 28, 56, 60, 68, 85, 89, 91, 99, 107, 111, 113, 119, 126, 127, 128, 129, 133, 135, 138, 139, 140, 144, 151, 161, 164, 169, 170, 177 (*see also* Logos)
  as character, 54-55, 67
  as idea, 124
  as Scripture, 107, 127, 138, 139, 164, 165 (*see also* Scripture)
  concepts of, 2, 8, 9, 13, 16, 17, 19
  creating, 9, 12, 74, 133
  Incarnate, 9, 10, 12, 99, 103, 117, 118, 127, 133
  in Gospel of St. John, 8
  in Milton's poetry, 173
  inner, 4, 9, 10, 11, 12, 13, 20, 30, 42, 48, 74, 75, 90, 97, 99, 106, 107, 111, 114, 122, 125, 135, 145, 161, 164, 168, 169, 170
  written, 28, 115

Ziff, Larzer, 181